Copyright 2001 by Ray Petit

First Edition

Cover Design by Ray Petit

Digital scanning and image editing

by Heidi Cummings

Library of Congress Cataloging-in-Publication Data

Printed in the United States of America

ISBN# 0-9713112-0-X

i

ABOUT THE AUTHOR

As war clouds darkened over Eastern Europe in the late 1930's and before the Japanese committed their "act of infamy," the United States initiated a military draft. The 18 to 20 something able Americans went to their draft boards and enlisted. The author, then living on a farm in northwestern Pennsylvania, enlisted in the U.S. Army Air Corps in October, 1941, and attended radio school in Scott Field, Illinois. In May, 1942, he was sent to New Orleans to join the 309th squadron of the 31st Pursuit Group. The 31st and the 1st Pursuit Groups were formed from Eddie Rickenbacker's WW I "Hat In The Ring" Pursuit Group. The 31st was building its strength for overseas combat duty. The Pursuit Group designation was changed to Fighter Group in May, 1942. They left for the European Theater of Operations in June, 1942. In England they were the first American Group to be trained by Royal Air Force pilots to fly the British Spitfire in the 8th Air Force. A 309th Squadron pilot was the first American to shoot down a German FW-190 in the European Theater. The Group was a part of the Dieppe Raid against the coast of France and later, the North African invasion on November 8, 1942. In the Mediterranean Theater of Operations, as part of the 12th Air Force, they provided air and ground support for the landings in Sicily and Italy. The Group changed airplanes to P-51 Mustangs when they became part of the strategic 15th Air Force in April, 1944 in central Italy, based in San Severo.

By the end of the war, the 31st Fighter Group became the highest scoring Fighter Group in the Mediterranean Theater of Operations. They received two Distinguished Unit Citations and fifteen campaign streamers during the period covered by this journal. The 31st still exists today as the 31st Fighter Wing in Aviano, Italy. The Wing earned the first Outstanding Unit Award in the history of the United States Air Force.

The 309th Fighter Squadron is now based at Luke AFB, Arizona flying F-16 Falcons.

Attitude Is Everything

WWII From My Vantage Point

by

Ray Petit

1941 AC Pvt. Ray E. Petit
Serial No.13038668

See Page 84 for full journal entry

iv

Dear Reader:

This book is non-fiction, all of it. It's an account of my three years overseas during WW II in the U.S. Army Air Corps in the European Theater of Operations---England, Africa, Sicily and Italy. If you expect three years of *Saving Private Ryan* action, you'll be disappointed with this. Chances are, if you are disappointed with reading some of it, we were probably bored also.

If you weren't lucky enough to have been part of *The Good War*, this account may convince you the tedium and discomforts and other things that accompany wars was a small price if it gives us the freedoms we have today.

Wars are serious business, what with the fear of death and real death, the valor and the squalor, the ingenuity and the improvisation, the defeats and the victories. Amongst all of that, they who are curious will find time to seek out art and architecture, music and dance, beauty and romance, solace and fulfillment. When you finish reading this little book, you will appreciate all of the above and understand why---Attitude Is Everything---earns cover space.

If your knowledge is in things other than airplanes, the Air Force (Air Corps in WWII) is about airplanes. When this book was written besides patrol, reconnaissance, training and a few othes, the important planes in WWII were bombers and fighters. The bombers carried the bombs to the targets and the fighters helped them get there and back safely. And fighter pilots strafed targets when they weren't busy protecting the bombers. Enough praise cannot be accorded these pilots and crews. They were all on the *imaginary front lines*, so to speak, where their bombs were dropped, on every mission. Supporting these courageous warriors were the ground support personnel such as mechanics, armorers, radiomen and others. It was our job to "keep 'em flying."

You'll find many journal entries reported simply and briefly what was happening. One simply said, "We lost our CO today." How stoical and unemotional war incidents become. One mentioned that Ralph Apple and I were strafed as we were returning from breakfast at a field kitchen near the Cassino (Italy) beachead. Another that Leroy Marsh and I wriggled into the ball on the very top of Saint Peter's Cathedral in Rome. Another when Marsh and I climbed to the top of the leaning tower of Pisa, trying to spot a field kitchen, a place to eat that night. You'll also notice changes in how we talked then and now. Things in the new millennium are *cool* or *awesome* when they were *swell* then, sometimes three times in one paragraph.

But let me back up and tell you a little about the guts of this book. It's really a log, a journal kept for unknown reasons from June 3, 1942 to the end of the war in Europe in May, 1945 when I returned to the States. It's not a diary with daily entries, as wars make that difficult. The entries were scribbled on pages of Lord Baltimore Service tablets, as noted nearby. The log came back to the States with me, on the bottom of my foot locker, where it remained for over 35 years. Most of us didn't talk much about our war experiences. When I was recuperating from one of my operations, I took it out and typed it single spaced, and it covered 54 - 8½ x 11 pages, a surprising 27,000 words. But more surprising was the awe, the surprise of something sublime, something that was not anticipated when each entry was recorded.

Reading it over again, I sensed how much we had all benefitted from those individual events. We went into the fray naive high school graduates and returned worldly-wise... and proud.

CONTENTS

Since the book, Mein Kampf, outlined what Adolph Hitler had in mind, the Allies and Russia knew what they had to do to foil his mad schemes. Millions of men and women joined the military as millions more worked the home front in one gigantic all out successful effort.

Since wars are seamless, one has to be arbitrary in choosing chapter titles. My list is short.

31st Fighter Group
309th FIGHTER SQUADRON
8th•12th•15th AIR FORCES
DIEPPE RAID TO V-E DAY
WORLD WAR II CAMPAIGNS

Air Offensive, Europe	Anzio	Northern Apennines
Algeria-French Morocco	Rome-Arno	Rhineland
with Arrowhead	Normandy	Central Europe
Tunisia	Northern France	Po Valley
Sicily with Arrowhead	Southern France	Air Combat, EAME Theater
Naples-Foggia		

DEDICATED TO THOSE WHO SERVED

DEDICATED 3 SEPTEMBER 1996

A bronze plaque, designed by the author, is in the Memorial Garden of the Air Force Museum at Wright Patterson Air Force Base, Dayton, OH

On the left is a design of the British Spitfire flown by our first Squadron Commander, Major Harrison R. Thyng, and on the right a P-51 Mustang, flown by Major Victor E. Warford.

The journal entries in this book authenticate what is happening when military goals are carried out and later posted as campaigns, fifteen in this case.

A digitally enhanced picture of the 309th Fighter Squadron radio section taken somewhere in North Africa in 1943. The author appears to be the only one to have predicted accurately the popularity of the baseball cap found today on everyone.

Front row, kneeling, L to R
J.Pankratz, WI (deceased)
H. Bain, OK (deceased)
N. Rieck, IA
J. McKay, PA (deceased)
Front row, standing, L to R
L. Powell, AK (deceased)
R. Savage, MA
V. Lee, OR
E. Guzzanato, WI

Back row, L to R
C. Taylor, CA
L.Linck, WI (deceased)
B. Parsley, IL
B. Harvey, ND (deceased)
L. Marsh, CA (deceased)
W. Shearin, NC
W. Pemberton, OR (deceased)
R. Petit, PA

Radiomen in a WW II Fighter Squadron tested and retested, installed and removed and maintained vital VHF radio communications between the pilot and other pilots and with the ground. The smiles attest one should try to enjoy what you are doing, wherever.

Missing from photo: R. Apple, CO; Lee Newell, NY; L. Keefer, IL; N. Mann, CA (deceased); G. Gilcrease, LA; D. Kipp, WA; D. Newman, CA; C. Ruess, NJ (deceased); C. Molchan, CO; O. Burkowski, NY (deceased).

Pilots of the 31st Fighter Group returned to Westhampnett for dedication of Memorial

On September 26, 1987 the above memorial stone was dedicated at our old Westhampnett Air Base outside Chichester, Sussex County, England. See pages 17 & 28. Lt. General Albert Clark represented the 31st Fighter Group at the dedication.

309th Fighter Squadron, Christmas time, 1942 in North Africa.
Some 200 noncommissioned officers and 21 pilots and seven non-flying officers.
Author is encircled upper right.

———◆———

This book is dedicated to
humble ancestors for shared genes
whose curious and optimistic mien and
resolute perseverance has resulted in publishing
this bit of military history some 59 years
after I made the original
journal entries.

———◆———

WW II From My Vantage Point

Chapter One
1942

June 3rd, 1942 . . .

This evening, with full field equipment and two barracks bags, we boarded a train in Fort Dix, New Jersey, for Brooklyn, to board a ship for overseas duty. We arrived in New York City about 11:00 p.m. and carried and dragged our bags about a mile to the ferry boat. This boat took us up the Hudson River, past the overturned Normandie, and on to where our ocean-going ship was berthed. This ship, to our amazement, turned out to be the largest ship afloat ... England's *Queen Elizabeth*. Needless to say, I hadn't ever experienced anything like this before. The immense size of this great ship one can't imagine. We boarded it at 2:00 a.m., June 4th.

June 4th . . .

When on board, we found we were to live (sleep and wait) in what was pre-war a large lounge. The beds are triple deckers and the quarters are very cramped. I don't know how we'll ever get out if we are torpedoed en route. It's three flights up to our life boat station. To sleep about 3:00 a.m. When we awoke about 8:00 a.m., we were still in the harbor.

My first glimpse of the world's largest city. Can't see much from here.

At 10:45 a.m., some tugs started pulling us out into the bay for my first ocean voyage. As we slowly steamed by the Lady With the Torch, and away from the U.S.A., Fred and Lida's son is a little apprehensive of what's in store for him. This is all so new and different ... ever coming back is the furthest thing from my mind now. Hope they don't worry. By nightfall, we were over the horizon, and it's all water now ... going to England, I guess.

June 5th ...

Water, water everywhere ... and none to take a shower with. I don't know when they'll turn on the water so we can wash. Very much confusion this morning. Didn't seem to be any system for feeding us. The mess hall is an enormous thing. It was the general dining room for peacetime use. I know it's possible to put our entire house in the dining room alone. The walls and ceiling are finished in walnut and around the sides are padded leather booths ... for the elite, I suppose. Class distinction is tossed to the wind at a time like this. A hotel-sized kitchen is off the dining room.

I went up on deck this forenoon to look around. There is a Navy blimp with us and that seems to be the extent of our escort. I don't feel so safe. I thought we'd have at least a couple cruisers along.

At noon, I was able to get a few boiled potatoes and cabbage. It's surprising what one can eat when hungry. I'm just finding this out. Much more to learn, I imagine. Bought some cookies, candy, etc., in the PX this P.M. It was a terribly long line to sweat out but eating in the mess hall also is a battle. This afternoon the blimp turned back. We are all alone now, and really buzzing along. The pilot changes the course of this great liner about 30 degrees every seven minutes so to fool any possibly present submarines. I understand it takes about that long for a submarine's crew to make sight adjustment, figure speed, direction, etc.

This is such a large ship that it doesn't roll much and there aren't many sick yet. I haven't thought much about it yet. Wait until we get out in the middle where the waves are large. The water is a very dark green now. Our wake shows up for miles behind. We wear kapok-filled life jackets constantly and have boat drills once a day, sometimes twice.

At lunch one day, a Major got up on a table and told us how dangerous an area we were in, and to eat the food even though we might not like it. (Nobody agreed with him.) Big lifeboats ... they are big! Big enough for 35 or 40 guys (and girls ... we have a bunch of nurses on here, too.) It's rumored there are between 15 and 18,000 troops on here. I suppose it's possible, the way everyone is packed in. I didn't bother eating in the mess hall tonight, ate cookies instead. Got in my middle bunk about 7:00 p.m. with my clothes on ... we're instructed to sleep this way ... put my head on my life jacket and went to sleep.

June 6th ...
Very big waves outside this morning. We're getting out into the middle, I think. Our squadron is pulling KP duty for the whole ship today. We run a shuttle service from the kitchen to the dining room. Smoked fish, porridge (typically British) for breakfast. Most of us aren't hep to this yet.

Didn't get up on deck today very much. The old girl rolled quite a bit at times today. I heard we went through a danger zone (submarine) at one point at dusk. I can't figure why the Captain blows the fog horn so often ... maybe so we won't run into anybody. I'd rather be quiet and try to sneak through.

Talked to one of the crew tonight and he set me right on a few things. The reason we don't have any escort is that no escorting vessel can keep up with the *Lizzy* when she opens up.

Anyway, there isn't much danger of submarine attack with all her speed. They can't keep up with us, but I'd think they could be waiting for us. That's why we change directions every seven minutes or so. The sailor said it would take more than one torpedo to sink her anyway because she's built in different compartments, which allows "sealing off" any damaged section. I hope he's right. I guess we really go fast at night, making it more difficult for subs. Our wake is very visible at night. The phosphorus in the salt water when stirred up glows like a firefly.

To bed, fully clothed, at 7:30 p.m. The lights stay on all night, just in case of some excitement. There are very strict black-out regulations on this ship. All portholes are closed at sundown, no one allowed on deck after then, and if you do sneak up, no smoking. There is no smoking in the sleeping quarters either.

June 7th ...

This seems like such a big world with so much water around and nothing else except sky. When I first saw flying fish, I thought we must be nearing land but we aren't, I guess. The air is much cooler now, we're getting farther north. A very strong wind blew today ... it just about blew Vic Peterson and me over the rail. Vic was with me in radio school in Scott Field but is in another squadron of the group. There seems to be engineers, infantry, airmen, nurses, a few English R.A.F. boys, etc., on here with us.

4

At times the waves are so large the *Lizzy* bobs around a bit. I saw a bunch of fellows sick, vomiting into their helmets. I haven't been sick yet, luckily. I don't have much of an appetite. The decks on this ship are so long. Such a ship as this is has more rooms than a hotel. The gunners fire occasionally, practice probably. I shot crap tonight and lost the little money I had ... fifteen dollars. It doesn't get dark until about 11:00 p.m. now so we must be up in the Arctic Circle. To bed at 11:30 p.m.

June 8ᵗʰ ...

The English cooks still persist in feeding us smoked haddock and porridge (without milk or sugar) for breakfast; boiled potatoes and cabbage for dinner, and cheese, bread and very bitter orange marmalade; and more smoked fish and tea for supper. It appears we are due for a change in diet when we get to England. We did get a couple apples at supper time that were probably brought over from the States with us.

I spent a lot of time out on the deck today, sniffing the salt air. We don't know how much longer our trip will be, but it's rumored it won't be much longer. Over the P.A. system that is on the boat, they relayed a program broadcast from Scotland, so we must be nearing there. It was bagpipe music, what sorrowful stuff. Quite a change from *Tune Town* in St. Louis. I wonder what the music and the girls, etc. will be like in England.

We're still going at breakneck speed and I like and feel proud that I'm on such a great ship and am doing what I am. An interesting thing about this ship is that it was under construction in Liverpool when England declared war on Germany. Foreseeing a possible bombing attempt to knock her out, the English immediately started her toward the

5

States, unfinished on the inside but able to navigate. While she was making a record time trip, German planes are supposed to have come over looking for her. In three days after she left England, she docked in New York City. Of course there was no submarine dodging then as now, but that's still record time. I understand this is the first time she's been back to England since she left unfinished. She's been making States to Australia, etc. runs.

We are in dangerous waters now and at 2:00 a.m., lifeboat drill is scheduled for tomorrow morning. Clothes on again tonight. I took a salt water shower today. Wow, is that saltwater cold! Soap doesn't lather too well either. Fresh water is on at the drinking fountains at different times of the day, and is on in the wash rooms in the mornings. More confusion on this ship ... so many troops and everything so new to all of us. To bed at 7:00 p.m.

June 9ᵗʰ ...
We all piled out at 2:00 a.m. this morning for that boat drill we knew was coming. We groped around in the dark, running into each other, falling down and experiencing the other mishaps that would prevail at something like this. No lights on and the job of finding one's lifeboat station out of a score or more. More fun. After about an hour of confusion, we were allowed to go back to bed until 6:00 a.m.

After breakfast this morning (porridge, etc.) we had to straighten things up and partially pack. It looks like we'll be sighting land before long.

There is so much that bewilders me at the present time ... such as, what is England like? Is there much danger of being bombed? Where in England are we going? Will I like England? Will we be able to go to London? ... etc., etc.

At about 5:00 p.m. we sighted land, the first in five days. It sure looked good. Some R.A.F. boys aboard said it was the northern tip of Ireland. At about the same time we sighted land, some fighter planes came out to escort us in ... *Spitfires*, they were. Surely was a pretty sight to see them buzz the ship, real low to the water. As we pulled closer to land and things took a definite shape and color, it looked pretty nice. We went up the River Clyde past many, many cruisers and other ships of all sizes, and cast anchor out in the middle of the river. There are many barrage balloons around to keep the Germans from coming in low and strafing. Thousands of sea gulls flying about.

No one seems to be getting off yet so I guess we'll be staying aboard another night. Anyway, we can see land. Got a lecture on the importance of the blackout once we get on land. We might get bombed, we are told. Serious business now. Got a haircut by one of the crew. Before I could say 'boo', my sideburns were gone. Oh, well, if that's what they do over here, I won't look out of style, I guess. Went to bed at 10:00 p.m., clothes off, the sun shining outside.

June 10ᵗʰ ...

We got up early today, preparatory to disembarking, I guess. Anyway, we spent the day on deck, just looking around. The sun shone some today but clouds seem to dominate the sky most of the time. At about 8:00 p.m. we left the *Queen* by a smaller boat for shore, carrying both barracks bags, field bag, gun, etc.

The little town they took us to was Greenock, the country, Scotland. Land seemed pretty solid when we stepped ashore. At the railway station here, we boarded some railway coaches. These are much different than our coaches back home in that, instead of having a door at each end and all the seats more or less in the same space, they (each coach) are divided into separate compartments with room for six people in each one. A door leads from each compartment to the outside. The platforms at the stations are high, so one can step from the coaches onto it. All is much different from ours.

About 10:00 p.m. we pulled out of this little Scottish town for a town in Shropshire County, England. The people in the towns we went through waved at us and seemed very happy we are here. I don't think there have been many Americans here before us. At dusk we had to close all the windows and the blinds for fear some light might shine out. We sat up all night and most of us didn't sleep much. It got quite cold before morning and Nolan Mann, four others and I put in a very miserable night in our compartment. I imagine the others were the same.

June 11ᵗʰ ...

We stopped at quite a large city this morning about dawn. There were some English soldiers at the station who gave us each a corned beef sandwich and a cup of coffee. Their coffee is different from ours I notice. We bought a morning paper and how small they are ... about 14" by 20" and only six or eight sheets to each paper. Looks like they may contain plenty of news though. After being here a few minutes we left and about 10:00 a.m. arrived at a little station out in the country. From here we rode in lorries (trucks) to the Airdrome where we are to stay for a while.

When we got to the bivouac area we were viewed with skepticism by the troops there. We had quite a time comparing and exchanging coins. I understand a shilling is worth twenty cents, a pound $4.00, etc. We are to sleep in four-man tents, and eat at one of the English mess halls. We were issued three blankets and a cot from the English.

From where we are camped on this hill, we can look over a very typical English countryside. Its hedges, thatched-roof houses, narrow roads, grain fields, etc. all are visible from here. In the background, we can see the town of Wellington and, behind that, the Wrekin Mountain. Incidentally, we can also see from here a W.A.A.F. camp. W.A.A.F., or Women's Auxiliary Air Force, is as the name implies, a service for women. They wear blue uniforms and look okay. Surely looks funny to see women soldiers. I guess these people are all out in this war effort.

We took a shower of ice water after we settled and then went to chow. The meal wasn't very exciting. My anticipation of a different diet is materializing. Kidneys cooked with cabbage, lettuce, bread and bitter orange peel marmalade, a pudding and tea for supper. There's a show in the mess hall tonight. I'm quite tired, didn't sleep much last night, so I guess I'd better go to bed early. All of us are sort of worn out from the trip. We'll perk up tomorrow, I think.

June 12th ...
We slept in this morning, until 8:00 a.m. It seems to be the English way, getting plenty of sleep. Anyway, we don't have any planes yet and therefore not much to do. For breakfast we had porridge (no milk), bread and orange marmalade, smoked fish and tea. For dinner, a thin piece of mutton, boiled potatoes (skins on), lettuce, a fairly good bread pudding with dressing, bread (all bread is whole wheat) and tea. For supper, kidney soup, boiled potatoes and cabbage, bread and the bitter marmalade, a slice of pudding-type cake, and tea. I don't know if I'll lose weight on this diet or not, surely is different from what we had in the States, but I like the whole wheat bread.

There is something like our PX here, they call it the Naffy.

Naffy really is N.A.A.F.I., or Navy, Army, Air Force Institute. At the Naffy we can buy chocolate (much different than ours,) soap, shaving supplies, soft drinks, tea, cakes, etc. The bulk of their business seems to be in tea and cakes. We went there before the show. The show was an old American film of about 1938 vintage.

We walked up from the mess hall to where we are camped on top of a hill overlooking the valley before the Wrekin. It was about 10:00 p.m. and the sun hadn't set yet. There was a big blackjack game going on in the area but I didn't indulge. In bed by 11:00 p.m. Seems to be planes flying over all the time. I hope they are friendly....

June 15th ...

We were told this morning we are to go to the airfield every day (one-half mile) and see what we can learn from the English. We are to have some English instructors attached to us until we are able to operate alone. I understand we aren't going to have the same planes *(Aircobras)* that the Group had in the States, but instead British *Spitfires*. Very nice ship, I guess.

Went to the Naffy tonight with Nolan Mann and then to Wellington. This is a typical little English village about six miles from here. It was the first town I had been to. We rode in on a bus that makes a nightly trip from the 'drome' to the town. Of course we went in on the "wrong" side (left) of the road. I was surprised to see how narrow and winding the streets were. Some of the streets in the middle of town are barely wide enough for two-way traffic. The people walk in the middle of the street. Looks peculiar ... of course, the sidewalks are only about four feet wide.

We test-hopped the beer just to see how it compared to ours back in the States. Sadly, it is served at room temperature, flat, tasteless, etc. Don't like it much. We found a *Hi-Y Club* where we got tea and cakes.

There are two theaters in town, both fairly nice ones. We went to one and saw *Yank In the R.A.F.*, quite an old show but new over here. Here's a peculiar feature about their "cinemas" ... the most expensive seats are in the balcony. The balcony isn't as far away from the screen as in the shows in the States. The seats down closest to the screen are the cheapest ones. From front to rear to balcony, the prices are one shilling (twenty cents,) one and six (thirty cents,) two shilling (forty cents,) balcony two and six (fifty cents) and the best balcony seats are three shillings (sixty cents.) Prices are sort of expensive but this is one of the few entertainments left for the people. The "pictures", as they call them here, get a good play.

Got back about 11:30 and it's still light out. England is a very peaceful place so far. Disregarding the constant hum of aircraft, there is a quiet atmosphere that is always present. I imagine in peace time, this is an easygoing place to live.

June 22ⁿᵈ ...

Tonight a few of us went to a little village about two miles from here called High Ercal. There is a little cracker-box dance hall there and a dance was being held. It was quite different from *Tune Town* in St. Louis. Music was furnished by a record player.

The English girls dance a little different than we do. They rate their music as waltz, fox trot, quick step, and a dance similar to our schottische. The English girls are very friendly and seem nice. I walked one back to the Waffery after the dance. It was just dark when I got back to camp. We will soon have a full moon here. Nights are quite cool.

11

June 26ᵗʰ . . .
Nolan Mann and I got up at 6:30 a.m. and went to chow.
We don't do this every morning as the breakfasts aren't that
good. Only a dozen or so go down to eat every morning. It is
rumored we may have our own mess hall before long. I sure
hope so.
    Went to the Naffy after supper and then to another dance
in the little village. Met a little WAAF tonight. She liked to
dance with me, thought I looked like Franchot Tone. Asked
me to come over tomorrow night and go for a walk with her.
These girls are much different than American girls in that they
are not coy. If they think they'd like to go out with a guy again
they plainly hint as to it. I think I prefer the American plan.
    Got back to camp in time to join a big blackjack game.
With the sun setting about 11:30 p.m., and a full moon, we
were able to play until 1:00 a.m. without a torch (flashlight.)

June 27ᵗʰ . . .
    The Queen of England and General Spaatz visited our
field today. I saw them go by. All the different types of
airplanes that are stationed at the field were lined up for
inspection. One type that seems to be popular with the R.A.F.
here is the *A-20 Boston* that has a million candlepower light in
the nose. It is called the *Havoc* by the English. The *Havoc* is
used in conjunction with two *Hurricanes* for night fighting.

June 29ᵗʰ . . .
    Went to a dance near the mess hall tonight and met a
beautiful blonde English WAAF. Seems like a nice kid. I have
a date for a night this week.

July 2ⁿᵈ 1942 . . .
Took the blonde bombshell to Wellington to a show
tonight. We had a sandwich first and afterwards went to an
exclusive (for this town) Pub for a scotch and soda. We went
back on the airdrome bus which was filled with soldiers, and
I had to hold her. Got back to camp about dark.

July 4ᵗʰ . . .
Had another dance tonight. Independence Day ...
everyone, the British and the Yanks (now friends) had a good
time. Saw the blonde again.

July 7ᵗʰ . . .
Today Nolan Mann and I got a three-day pass for London.
We left Wellington about 9:00 a.m. on the train. On the way,
we went through Wolverhampton and Birmingham, and
arrived in London shortly after noon. We got a room at the
Washington Club on Curzon Street, just off Picadilly. The
room had very soft beds and an adjoining bathroom ... a really
nice room and only a shilling (twenty cents.) We got some
sandwiches at the snack bar and read some States papers in
the huge lounge. We inquired as to what there is to see
tomorrow and decided to take a tour of London in a taxi for ten
shillings each. Should see quite a bit of this famous city.

We asked about a dance hall and were told a place by the
name of *Covent Gardens* would be our best bet. We went and
had a very good time. *Covent Gardens* is now a large
ballroom but was an Opera House in peacetime. The Royal
Box is boarded up but the other balcony seats serve as a place
to sit and watch the dancers. The bandstand is in the center of

the ballroom and revolves around with the dancers. Incidentally, two bands play alternately, a half hour each. Both bands are top notch London orchestras with a solid beat. Over the bandstand is a crystal ball that revolves and when a light is shone on it, it reflects giving the impression of falling snow. Very nice! The girls there outnumbered the fellows about five to one, so we danced quite a bit. I met a girl, Joy, by name, and took her home. She hadn't been out with a Yank yet so she had a number of questions to ask. I went with her in a two-decker tram (bus) out by the River Thames to her parents home on the outskirts of London. London is completely blacked out at night except for air raid shelters and subways. There are dim signs pointing to these. When I started back, the subways had stopped running and I had miles and miles to go to the Washington Club. My first night in blacked-out London. By inquiring of Bobbies and others, I got back O.K.. I stopped in at one of the two restaurants that stay open all night on the way back and got some toast and cocoa. Got to bed about 1:30 a.m.

July 8ᵗʰ ...
Nolan and I got up this morning, had breakfast ... eggs, cereal, coffee and toast ... in the snack bar and at 9:00 a.m. left in a taxi for our tour of London. The mature taxi driver said he had driven Franchot Tone around town once, and that I reminded him of Tone. He drove us around stopping occasionally and explaining different things. Among other places, we saw Buckingham Palace, Westminister Abbey, Big Ben, the badly blitzed part, St. Paul's Cathedral, the little Curiosity Shop, London Bridge, the Tower of London, the Fish Market on the Thames, Waterloo Bridge, Houses of Commons and Parliament, 10 Downing Street, Scotland Yard Headquarters, Thames River, some original buildings of the

14

old London fire, Cripple Gate Church (William Penn was married here,) and some of the large theaters of London. We got back from the tour about noon, so we went to the *American Eagle Club* and got the first Coca Cola, hamburgers and cream puffs that we've had since we left the States. This club was about the first one formed for Americans in London. It has a lounge, a record player, reading room, etc. It's O.K.! This afternoon and night we went to a couple shows. To bed about 10:00 p.m.

July 9th . . .
This morning, we got up with nothing definite in mind to do so we decided to just slum about. In the forenoon, we rode in different directions in double decker trams and subway cars. We went out into the suburbs and back. In the afternoon, we went out to Richmond (an outskirt district) to a large rink and went ice skating. We rented some shoe skates and had quite a time. At about 3:00 p.m. we went back to the Club, checked out and went to Paddington Station to leave for High Ercal. We sat up all night long in a coach with a couple WAAF's. We didn't say much to them and tried to sleep. We got back to Wellington in the morning and caught a truck to camp. Got back in time for roll call, the first roll call since we left Fort Dix.

July 11th . . .
We are still going to the line and boning up, and our pilots are flying much. Back of our flight line are a couple canteens (Naffys) and we go there a couple of times a day for tea, cookies, and Spam sandwiches. There is also a farm there where we can get a glass of fresh milk occasionally.

July 14th ...

Helped remove a harness from a *Spit* today, my first try. Quite a job.

July 16th ...

Our cooks are setting up our own mess hall. Surely glad of that, maybe we can have some American food for a change.

July 17th ...

Had breakfast in our own mess hall this morning ... hot cakes, syrup, sausages and coffee. Every forenoon a Naffy truck drives around the flight line selling tea, cakes, etc. We all swarm around it and buy something. The English take time out for tea at 10:00 a.m. and 3:00 p.m.

I rode to a little dance hall tonight on the bus with some English women who said I was the first American they'd seen since World War I.

July 23rd ...

Went to another dance in the little village tonight. Some of the guys are buying bicycles to go to the line, town, etc. Very useful. I may get one later.

July 26th ...

I guess our pilots are getting enough experience now. Anyway, the rumor is that we are to move to the southeast coast to go on Ops. Got some American rations today ... candy, beer, cigarettes, etc.

July 31st ...

We were told today we are to leave tomorrow for a field near Chichester in Sussex County. It's in the southeast, not too far from London. Good.

August 1ˢᵗ 1942 . . .
Left this morning by train for Chichester and arrived there
at 3:00 p.m. The field we'll be at is Westh ampnett and it's
about three miles from the city of Chichester. As we came
through the town, it looked nice. We (sixteen guys) moved
into a half-moon roofed, corrugated steel hut called a Nissen
hut. There is a stove in the middle and a window in either end.
Today was Saturday so we decided to go into the town at
night. Norm Rieck, Larmon Powell, Jerry Pankratz and I
walked in. We found a nice dancing place and I met a very
cute little blonde in a yellow dress, Margaret Brown. She
seems nice, maybe a bit skeptical. I walked with her to her
home and made a date for next week.

August 2ⁿᵈ . . .
Our *Spits* came in today from High Ercal. After some
confusion, they were dispersed according to flights. The
flight I'm in is A Flight and over on the other side of the field
from where we are sleeping. I hope we can move over there ...
there is another Nissen hut there.

August 3ʳᵈ . . .
Went to Chichester tonight to see the little blonde. Met
her mother ... nice. They have a cozy little home,
immaculately clean, everything in order. We went to a
show, an old one. It cost sixty cents each, most of this being
tax, I'm told. Went for a walk afterwards and compared
traits, characteristics, customs and so forth. We are both
sold on our particular countries, I can see that. At a mild
suggestion, I was induced to go in and see her again soon.
She's a cute kid, nineteen.

17

We've been leased an English mess hall. It is quite large and somewhat on the order of the mess halls in the States. It is located about a mile from the line but I don't mind the walk. The food we get is from both countries and not too much of either. There's an English Naffy near the mess hall where we can get beans and toast dinners, tea, cakes, soap, shaving cream, etc. We eat there when our meals aren't sufficient.

Our pilots go up on what is called "squadron formations." It isn't operational, just practice, usually twelve at a time. The field here is quite large, a grass one, with an asphalt "perimeter" running completely around it. Forty millimeter *Bofors* (ack-ack guns,) are at different points around the field, also barbed wire entanglements.

These Brits are surely ready for a possible invasion. As far north as High Ercal was, they still had all the hedges along the roads interlaced with barbed wire, tank traps, tank blockades, block houses, mine fields, etc. Everything complete. I notice down here there are many more home guards who go on watch every night. Also, air raid wardens and fire wardens. Margaret's dad goes on watch regularly. I went in again last night.

Some of us in A Flight moved to the Nissen hut over by the A Flight line today. We changed places with some B Flight guys who were there. I like it much better here ... it is about fifty feet from A Flight's Radio shack, which is in the same building as our Orderly Room, Operations, Intelligence Office and Adjutant's Office ... very convenient for getting our mail, formations, work, etc. I am assigned four planes about three hundred yards from our radio shack. Went into Chi again last night. Very serious, these English girls.

August 8th ...
Many of the guys have gotten bicycles. I'm looking for one now.

August 11ᵗʰ ...

I bought a used bicycle from a Canadian today. Canadian ground troops are stationed in this area also. It is a fairly good one. I plan to take it apart and grease it, and fix it up. It cost five pounds, or $20.00. That seems like quite a bit of money but new ones cost as high as $45.00. I need a bicycle to ride to town, to chow, on the line, etc.

August 16ᵗʰ ...

Our pilots go on sweeps occasionally over France. Sometimes they escort bombers. Different times we are on "instant" alerts. When we are, and "raiders" are reported, the pilots come riding out of Ops on their bicycles, the crew chiefs start up the *Spits*, anyone helps them get on their parachutes,they are strapped in and off they go in a cloud of dust. Our C.O. has shot down a *Jerry* on a scramble mission like this.

These British have a foolproof system in regard to communications. I think it's nearly impossible for a German plane to get in here without being spotted.

August 19ᵗʰ ...
Day of Dieppe Raid

We were up this morning at 4:00 a.m., calling in the planes for an early mission. Although we didn't know then, it turned out to be a raid on the coast of France at Dieppe. Canadian ground troops carried out the assault and our pilots flew at least four missions each. One pilot came back and said planes were falling into the Channel like quarters flipped into a rain barrel. Two of our pilots had to bail out but they got back O.K..

Margaret Bourke White and other International News

19

Photo people were taking pictures. One took one of me hanging up some laundry on our clothes line .. to show the Yanks are in the thick of things, I guess. He said it would be in papers in the States. Also had a movie taken, four of us by a *Spit*. News on the radio said it was a successful raid and not intended as a second front, as reported by the Germans.

August 29th . . .
   I stayed in the hut tonight. Last night completed a seven night engagement in Chichester. I'd better slow down a bit. This girl is always planning some place to go, and when she asks me to come in, I agree to it. They have me come in after a show, dance or whatever, for tomato and cheese sandwiches, cookies, tea, fruit, etc. I know their food is rationed and try to refuse it, but it's no use. Such hospitality! I have some English chocolate bars that I've gotten through ration that I don't particularly want. Think I'll give them to these people. I know they will appreciate them as they get only so much per family a week. Candy, canned foods, shoes, clothing, etc. are all strictly rationed here. One could nearly say, everything is rationed here.

September 3rd 1942 . . .
   It was my day off today so Ralph Apple and I went to Chi and bought some things ... clothes pins, a hot plate, glass wash board, apples, tomatoes, etc. We already have an electric flat iron in the billet that we can press our clothes with daily. Now, with the hot plate, we can heat water to do our washing with, shave, make cocoa, etc. We can send our laundry out if we wish, but it is so convenient here that we prefer to do it ourselves. At all times, there is at least one guy in the billet who is either pressing or washing clothes. I think we must be

the best dressed section on the field. This is a very neat setup here. I wonder how long we'll be here?

September 4th . . .
Our food is getting better, more things from the States. A lot of it is dehydrated, potatoes, carrots, beets, corn and prunes. We go to the Naffy occasionally for beans, toast and tea.

September 5th . . .
Got cigarettes, candy, peanuts, tooth paste, shaving cream rations today. We get this kind of ration once in a while.

September 7th . . .
Tonight after the dance at *Kimball's* (where I first met Margaret,) she had me in to a mushroom supper. Besides mushrooms, we had toast, tomatoes, Spam and tea, and chocolate cake. I hadn't had any mushrooms in a long time and they were delicious. She knew I liked them back in the States.

September 8th . . .
I took in 24 bars of English chocolate to the Brown's tonight. They were over-joyed, said it was a couple months ration for them. I like to talk to Mr. Brown, he is so optimistic about the war. Says we can't lose. He claims the *Spitfire* is the best plane. I guess he's right.

Had an alert as I was leaving. Scores of searchlights piercing the sky. We could hear bombs dropping, maybe on Portsmouth. Margaret was worrying about me getting back to the field all right. I made it O.K..

September 10ᵗʰ ...

Had another alert tonight. I guess they bombed Portsmouth or Bognor. Heard one astray bomb drop near here. As the *Jerries* came back across to France, they went about over us and the *Bofors* around here opened up. I think they knocked one down. We have raids like this occasionally. The air raid siren in Chichester always goes and besides that there is a P.A. system in each billet to warn us of enemy aircraft approaching. The field hasn't been raided yet though we've seen vapor trails directly overhead, reconnaissance, I guess. The day following a raid like tonight, BBC says, "A few raiders were over East Anglia during the night. Bombs were dropped at scattered points with little damage. Few casualties were reported." It seems to be a stock statement.

September 12ᵗʰ ...

Went to a dance across from *Kimball's* tonight at a place called *The Assembly Room.* Had a pretty good time. With a strict blackout enforced, a place like that gets pretty stuffy. Burke and his girl were there with us.

September 13ᵗʰ ...

I worked on my bicycle today. The brakes were getting poor and it needed greasing. At dusk, Ernie Whitman and I took a nice ride out through the countryside. Rode over to the big airdrome at Tangmere, through some little villages, and home by dark. We went to the Naffy and had some beans and toast before going to the billet.

September 14ᵗʰ ...

Ralph Apple, Vance Lee, Oscar Burkowske and I rode nine miles to Bognor Regis tonight. It is a town on the Channel and has a large ball room. It was a resort town in

22

peace time, the same as Brighton, which is east from us some on the coast. There were many Canadians there but we were able to get a few dances. Burke and I walked a couple girls part way home. Apple and Lee made dates for next week with two. We rode back in the fog, nine miles without resting. Got back a bit after 1:00 a.m.

September 17th . . .
Today Burke and I got permission to be absent for a couple days and we started for London. We left on the train at 2:30 p.m. from Chi and got to London about 5:00. Burke hadn't been there before. We got rooms in the Washington Club Annex as we couldn't get a room where Nolan Mann and I had once before. Since so many American soldiers are arriving in England now, and they all want to visit London, it makes it difficult to get a room in the Club proper.

After we got the room we went out on the street since he had not seen anything in London. We visited the American Bar of the Piccadilly Hotel as well as some other night clubs and went to *Covent Gardens* about 9:00 p.m. It was the same as when Nolan and I were there in the past, i.e., many girls, two bands playing alternately, the revolving bandstand, the crystal ball, jump music and sort of an American atmosphere. This might be attributed to the many American soldiers who were there. We both danced quite a bit and went out for cocoa and toast before going back to the Club Annex.

September 18th . . .
We went to the *American Eagle Club* this morning, drank some cokes, ate cream puffs, etc. And then went riding on the subways, trams, etc. We went to Westminster Abbey, saw Buckingham Palace, and other sights. We bought some things. I got a cigarette lighter and Burke got a cigarette case.

23

We went to a stage show in the afternoon, *No Orchids For Miss Blandish*. It was the first English stage play I had seen and I really enjoyed it. Little is barred in these plays. We ate supper at the *Eagle Club* and then went to Victoria Station to get the train for Chichester. We got to the billet about 1:00 a.m.

September 20th . . .
Today I learned my watch is at the A.P.O. and I will have to go on the mail truck to get it. Mom sent it to me after getting it from Fort Dix. I left it there to be fixed when I left for overseas. I'm to go to get it tomorrow.

September 21st . . .
Went on the mail truck today and got my watch. As I was unwrapping it, it fell from the case onto the running board and now it refuses to run. Such luck. On the way up and back, we went through South Hampton. This is a fairly large city and sections of it have been completely leveled by German aircraft.

September 22nd . . .
Today I got off early in the afternoon and went to Margaret's home. She had planned to go on a trip by bus to a little town on the Channel, a few miles from here. Before we went we climbed to the top of the bell tower in Chichester. This is reputed to be one of the few cathedrals in England that has a separate bell tower. It has very large bells and beautiful sounds. At the little Channel town, we laid on the grass and watched little kids go wading in the Channel. The water is quite cool now. We didn't go to a show when I got back, and I didn't promise to come in again soon. It is rumored we are to leave in the near future and I don't want her to be carrying a torch for me. She knows I'm here to help fight a war and will

have to see me leave her before long. We like each other more than a little.

... C' est la guerre!

September 25th ...
We are marching around the perimeter occasionally and skirmishing around in the woods with guns, etc. Getting in shape or marking time for something. Our pilots aren't flying much anymore. Today we had a mock battle on top of the racetrack hill. It rained and we got wet.

September 27th ...
Today Burke and I went in and got the girls and took a train to Portsmouth. That town is really beat up, about the worst I've seen, including London. We went to a show and had supper and came back. Margaret and I had a little spat, still she wants me to come back again. I doubt that I will.

September 30th ...
Our squadron has been divided into three echelons now. Today P4, the first echelon, had a dinner of canned rations, C ration, I think ... beans, etc. in one can and crackers, candy, coffee and sugar in another. That must be what we'll eat if our kitchen isn't set up sometime somewhere. I'm in the first echelon ... erp!

October 3rd 1942 ...
We are living a life of ease now. No work calls, no work, no restrictions. We stay in the billet much and read, play blackjack, press clothes, and the like. We work on equipment boxes some and plan to take apart our bicycles and pack and send them wherever we go.

October 5th ...

Oscar Burkowske, Ralph Apple, Vance Lee and I rode our bikes into Chi tonight. We always ride in close formation, and as fast as we can go. If one of us would ever spill, we all would. We went around Chi looking for a dance and couldn't find one so we went to a bar in a hotel. Later we went to a pub called the *White Swan* where they had some quadruple X ale. We know we're shipping out, so what the heck! We all had a great time drinking the stuff, or we thought we did at the time.

We left for the parking lot of the bikes. Burke was kicking over everything in his path. He kicked in a window of a basement apartment and we all had to run to get away from there before a Bobbie came. While we were running, I looked back and saw a Bobbie running after us with his torch (flashlight). Something told me he would catch us, so I stopped, turned around and started walking towards him. When he got to me, he stopped and asked if I had seen some Yanks running down the street. I said I wasn't sure and, at that point, I wasn't sure of anything. After walking around town a couple of times, we rendezvoused at the lot and started back for the base. There was no precision riding as in going into Chi but we did get back without further damage to anything or to us. Apple and I were the last to get to the billet. What a night!

Wonder where we are going when we leave here? I bought an air mattress earlier today.

October 7th ...

Some of the guys in the squadron went to Liverpool and brought back some Jeeps today.

26

October 8th . . .
Today we took our bicycles apart and packed them in boxes so we can have transportation wherever we go. We'll have to walk now.

October 10th . . .
Some ratings came out today. I made Corporal, that's $79.20 a month.

October 13th . . .
Still hanging around the billet, nothing much to do except to make equipment boxes and mark our barracks bags.

October 17th . . .
Got a letter from Margaret, wondering. In a return letter, I told her we were leaving soon and we did not know where we would be going, that I felt as she did, but it's a war.

October 18th . . .
Our squadron had a dance tonight in our mess hall. WAAFs and ATS girls were there. I danced a little and left early.

October 19th . . .
Really getting ready to leave now. Guess the fun and dancing are over for a while.

October 20th . . .
We were told today to pack our barracks bags. We put "non essentials" in a "B" bag and sent them on a truck. The things we need, like clothes, toilet articles, etc., we put in an "A" bag and we are to carry them with us. Mine is full to the

top and feels like it weighs 300 pounds. It's very quiet in the billet tonight. Tomorrow the first echelon leaves for ? ... I'm one of them.

October 21st ...

We assembled across from our billet this morning in echelons and were told we were going to a place that wouldn't be in our hands until we got there. Sounds interesting. The first echelon (P4) left in trucks for the train station in Chi, and from there we went up the east Channel coast through Brighton, London, Cambridge, New Castle, Edinburgh, Glasgow, etc. The barbed wire entanglements and other means of defense are certainly complete along the Channel. Traveled all night on the train, sitting up.

October 22nd ...

As it became light this morning, we are still going north with the Channel on our right. The pretty green valleys and rolling hills we saw, we decided was Scotland. At about 8:00 a.m., we stopped at a large town which was Edinburgh, and got some corned beef sandwiches and tea. We also got a couple sandwiches from our cooks that they had brought along from Westhampnett. We left there soon and in a short time we were back in Greenock, Scotland, at the same station we left from for High Ercal. After waiting around for a while, we boarded a ferry boat for a larger ship out in the bay. This boat is just a row boat compared to the *Lizzy*. It's the *Orbita* and quite a tub. This will turn out to be some trip, I think.

October 23rd ...

We are anchored out in the middle of the River Clyde, about where we were when we arrived from the States. Equipment and troops are being constantly loaded onto ships of all sizes, both American and English. There are quite a lot of boats anchored around us ... aircraft carriers, etc. Looks like it will be quite an excursion, lots and lots of vessels.

October 24th ...
I had the choice today of either having KP or guard duty while on the trip. I chose KP as I despise guard duty. So far, the food is typically English. It will undoubtedly be on a par with the food on the *Lizzy* ... in other words, not so good.

October 25th ...
This ship seems to be about loaded now but I doubt if all the others are. Much complicated loading on a trip like this ... what goes where and when to arrive is vital, I imagine. This river is buzzing with activity, ships of all descriptions here.

October 26th ...
I chose not to sleep in a hammock on this trip but to put my air mattress on the floor and sleep there. Burke has his on the floor, too. I can see already the air mattress is going to be valuable to me. We may be sleeping on the ground when we get where we're going, who knows?

October 27th ...
This morning when we went on deck we were moving out of the River Clyde with boats all around us ... looks like a big show coming up. Although I don't get sick enough to vomit, I don't exactly feel tip top, especially in this choppy water.

October 29th ...
On the *Orbita*, out in the ocean now with land leaving us. B-17s circling constantly.

November 1st 1942 . . .
   Quite a convoy this is. Supposed to be the biggest over here so far.

November 5th . . .
   We came through the Straits of Gibraltar and are now in the Mediterranean Sea. What a blue color. I threw a nickel in for good luck.

November 8th . . .
   This morning I went up on deck at about 4:30 a.m. as I was anxious to see what was about to happen. Occasionally we could see tracers from PT boats, etc. piercing the darkness. Saw some boat go by all lighted up. At daylight we pulled to within two miles of the shore and cast anchor. Small boats were skirmishing about, laying smoke screens. A few *Spits* flew overhead.
   The little village, Arzeu by name, looked nice against the brown countryside, especially not having been near land for about two weeks. We weren't allowed on deck for fear we might get in the way of the unloading operations. I sneaked up once anyway and hid behind a ventilator. In the little town I could hear machine gun fire. Makes you a little uneasy.
   We spent the forenoon in the day room listening to radio reports on the landing. About 2:30 p.m. we put on all our field equipment and left the *Orbita* via L.C.T., about 30 fellows in each one. The sea was quite choppy on the way in. At about fifty yards out, the landing craft ran aground, the end was opened up and off we went into the Mediterranean. It wasn't very cool but plenty salty. Nurses were walking ashore as well as soldiers.
   All kinds of equipment was being unloaded from the

landing craft. Bull dozers were making roads with little regard for the cottages that were along the water. Ack-ack guns were set up in different places. Our squadron assembled into three sections and we went back about 200 yards from the water and laid down our bed rolls (me on my air mattress). We were told we could eat one of our issued D rations (a candy bar) for supper. John McKay and I unrolled our bed rolls together and threw our pup tents over our beds. The wind was blowing, making it very difficult to sleep.

At about 10:00 p.m. we were awakened and told they expected paratroopers to be dropped where we were. Most of us got onto G.I. trucks and started for the airdrome. It was supposed to have been taken today by our paratroopers ... I hoped they did! We went through darkness for about two miles and finally drove into the courtyard of a palm-fringed estate. Our troops had commandeered it and were using it for Headquarters.

We stayed there for a short while as the radios squeaked out code as the operators tried to find out if the road to the airfield was in our hands. It was finally found that one road was open and we started out on that one. About eight G.I. trucks made the trip with a half-track between each one ... plenty of protection. As we rode along, we didn't realize how dangerous it might have been. It was cold cramped on the bottom of the truck. John McKay and I sat in the rear with our guns ready to fire in case we were fired upon.

November 9th ...
Last night we rode all night and slept little. At the graying of dawn we arrived at the gate of the airfield. At first it looked deserted and ominous. As it became lighter, we could see a few Frenchmen walking about. We stayed parked at the gate

about half an hour and then started again onto the field. We had gone about 200 yards when we heard a plane taking off. We stopped just as it flew over us. It dropped a 500 pound bomb that landed about 100 yards from where we were scrambling out of the trucks. The half-tracks opened up on it with their 50-caliber machine guns. We could see tracers go into it or near it, and on it went.

Everyone was nerved up at this point, our first exposure to any action of that kind, and we're running around in circles. We found out our planes were dispersed across the field so we started to walk across to them. We went by the crater of the bomb the Frenchman just dropped. It made quite a hole and knocked dirt through the side of a C-47 transport parked there.

When we got to our planes, we found a dirty but grateful looking bunch of pilots. We understood then what we had been told, that the field might not be taken when we got there. That was to happen many, many times in the months ahead as we went eastward in North Africa.

Since the pilots had fought their way into the field the previous day, they had been servicing the planes themselves and sleeping little. I changed a set in the Colonel's ship as well as helped other guys. I was super-tired at this point, no sleep since the previous morning and that all night ride. That was some ride.

As the sun came up behind the Atlas Mountains and the light rays shown through the dust-laden air, it was a very beautiful sight . . . my first sunrise in Africa. As our airborne planes circled above the field, we could see ack-ack puffs by them. That meant there were still unfriendly French anti-aircraft guns around. In the distance, over a hill, we could see smoke billowing upward. When our pilots came back, they said it was the other airfield, the large municipal one, La

Senia. They said the French were burning their hangars, planes and equipment.

As we were very hungry, about noon we ate a couple cans of C-rations. They tasted sort of good, but we were so starved. I heard some of the guys were confiscating tools, boots, etc., from the hangars so I decided to follow them. I got a pair of flying boots, silk gloves, parachute silk, tools, etc. I also got a stop watch from the cockpit of one of the fighter planes.

About 3:00 p.m., Vic Peterson and I were in the French Tech Supply looking at precision gauges and stuff when we heard a bunch of explosions outside. We ran out and we could see shells landing at the end of the field amongst some *C-47s* and some of the other squadrons' *Spitfires*. We realized then that the French Foreign Legion had artillery set up and were shelling us.

We all started running in different directions after our Tommy guns. At this time, we had seen few of our infantry troops and we wondered what was there to defend the field. Immediately our *Spits* took off to go strafe the artillery and tanks the Foreign Legion had put by the field. We stood awe-stricken and cheered as our planes, the ones we take care of, make pass after pass at the tanks, trucks, etc., not knowing what the best thing for us to do. Much dust was rising from the far end of the field. Our pilots destroyed a bunch of their tanks, and they turned back. We helped refuel the planes and they went out again and strafed remaining trucks and tanks.

We could see burning vehicles miles away on roads going up the mountains. An ironic part of this was that not enough ammunition or gas had been brought in yet from the beachhead where we had come in at Arzeu, so for the second attack we had to improvise. We drew gas from the *C-47s* that brought in the paratroopers and 20 m.m. ammunition came from French planes and armament shops. Our pilots saved the day for us and the airfield by quick thinking and straight shooting. Small arms fire hit some of our planes and one went down. The Major (C.O.) Flying it was returned by Arabs for some gold.

Our food is still C-rations and corned beef ... our kitchen will be set up in due time. Most of the guys haven't gotten here from the beach yet. Ralph Apple and I have our Headquarters in a baled straw stack — hope it doesn't cave in on us. The Chaplin is in part of the stack also. We had a formation tonight with Tommy guns and ammo. An expected counterattack was discussed but when a pilot came back, he said that as he flew over some tanks they waved a white flag. Some half-tracks will go up and bring them down. When we bedded down tonight I was so tired I couldn't sleep, then the constant firing of guns all night had something to do with it.

November 10ᵗʰ ...

Our planes went off at sunrise this morning, looking for ack-ack guns, etc. We were up and called them in before they left. Had heated C-rations and hot water to make chicle-coffee with. Some infantry came in today and more half-tracks, and they set up around the field. Some paratroopers are here, too, been here since the 8ᵗʰ. They caught hell when they came down from England.

We are having quite a time getting enough water to wash with and to drink. Just a canteen is all until we're sure of the local water here. We snapped up some tangerines down by the big (French) mess hall today. I'm told this was a big French Navy base.

These Arabs are funny looking to us, running around with baggy-seated pants, long outer garments and beards (men.) They go walking along the road barefooted, maybe a family at a time. The man first, then the wives and offspring trailing

34

behind and, often as not, a goat running along beside, blatting like hell. Two or three fellows . . . .

NOTE:

It seems there would be an explanation why an explicitly kept log would tail off as the above did, and there be no evidence of any entries for the entire month of December. But there is none! Certainly there were more Lord Baltimore Service Tablets in the pipeline from the States to Africa, and living conditions weren't all that bad for the next few weeks.

In any event, from the haystack with the frightened Chaplain, we moved to more permanent quarters nearer Oran, La Senia, on November 13th. Here we had use of a repair hangar and runway. Had our squadron pictures taken and our first Thanksgiving Day dinner afield.

Christmas was replete, too, with the same fare, even a Christmas skit involving our revered Colonel Thyng.

We eased into local commerce there to the delight of the Arabs and other hucksters who sold us everything from local fruits to "rare gems." Oran, which was little affected by the war (actually we had brought the war to them in November) happily served our more exotic needs for French perfumes and colognes. Also alabaster objects, cigarette boxes and jewelry of every description, while their beautiful harbor constantly disgorged war paraphernalia for use in accelerating the North African campaign.

So, as we adjusted to and tried another society, occasional entries began to appear, sketchy maybe but clearly enough to determine which way we were going. We were heading east ... and we were ready!

Chapter Two
1943

January 2nd 1943 . . .
Inspection by Colonel Dean today.

January 16th . . .
Went to Oran to buy some perfumes and gifts to send to the States.

January 20th . . .
Major Thyng and Captain Mitchem ran together today, damaged both planes. They weren't hurt.

January 23rd . . .
8th Army went into Tripoli today. Progress.

January 28th . . .
Carol Landis visited La Senia today with a cast.

January 30th . . .
308th returned from Casa Blanca, patrolling for President Franklin Delano Roosevelt.

February 6th 1943 . . .
Guys left for front, Thelepte, by air. Us soon.

February 11ᵗʰ ...
Martha Raye at show here. Sang *Honeysuckle Rose* . . .
with oomph!

February 12ᵗʰ ...
We're waiting to go. Sweating out planes, sleeping in radio
shack.

February 14ᵗʰ ...
Left at 10:30 a.m., this morning for Thelepte. Got to
Relizame in an hour and landed because of bad weather.

February 15ᵗʰ ...
Waiting for weather to clear to go on.

February 16ᵗʰ ...
Left at 10:00 a.m. this morning; turned back because of
weather. In air two hours

February 17ᵗʰ ...
Another day at Relizame sweating out the weather.

February 18ᵗʰ ...
Still sweating.

February 19ᵗʰ ...
Left at 10:30 a.m. In air an hour, landed at Blida, near
Algiers. Stayed in hangar all night.

February 21ˢᵗ ...
Weather O.K. today; left at 10:30 a.m. and got to
Telergma about noon.

February 22ⁿᵈ ...
Found out our outfit is at Youks-les-Bains.

February 26ᵗʰ ...
Left at 8:00 a.m. by trucks for Canrobert; got there at 10:00 a.m. Pitched our tent (Bob Savage, Harned Bain, Vance Lee and I.) Pup tents in the mud, connected up the radio.

February 27ᵗʰ ...
Went to Ambidia for steam bath, my first ... quite an experience. Good way to bathe. Made a plywood radio shack. Decided to sleep in it, too.

March 8ᵗʰ 1943 ...
Burke got orders for transfer today. Climbed a mountain for the first time. Colonel Thyng made executive officer for the Group.

March 9ᵗʰ ...
Went up the mountain again and cooked our dinner. Took pictures.

March 10ᵗʰ ...
Moved by truck to Youks les Bains, and set up portable radio shack.

March 16ᵗʰ ...
Went into town and bathed in old Roman baths.

March 19ᵗʰ ...
Went to Thelepte. We're not sleeping underground . . . . .

March 23rd . . .
Two lieutenants got shot down today, one came back. We went back for clothes at Youks. Our kitchen and Ops are underground.

March 24th . . .
Four missions today over Gabes and Sfax.

March 25th . . .
Three missions today. Captain Hill got a *FW-190*.

March 26th . . .
Two missions today with *B-26*s and *A-20*s.

March 27th . . .
Planning a big drive. Pilots briefed. A mobile outfit moved in for a day's show with International pilots, a Czech for C.O. We fooled the *Jerries* with *Spit IX*s.

April 1st 1943 . . .
Lost a Lieutenant today.

April 2nd . . .
Lost our first escorted bomber today. Bad.

April 3rd . . .
Some of the boys slept in today, and got hell!

April 5th . . .
Got raided today in daylight, and the *Jerries* hit some *A-20*s on the other side of the field. First time I've seen enemy planes close up on a daylight raid. More ahead . . . . .

April 6ᵗʰ . . .
Six missions today. Big show coming up. Some *A-20* boys bailed out. Got four new *Spit IXs*. Good deal.

April 7ᵗʰ . . .
Left Thelepte for Sbeitla by truck. Enemy planes over today. New strip being built . . . . .

April 9ᵗʰ . . .
Two of our pilots left today to become C.O.s in A-36 Group.

April 10ᵗʰ . . .
Sfax falls to 8ᵗʰ Army today.

April 12ᵗʰ . . .
Left this morning at 8:00 a.m. for La Sers. Another strip.

April 14ᵗʰ . . .
Heard about extension course from Penn State today that I want to take. Pressed for time ... don't know when I'll study.

April 17ᵗʰ . . .
Lt. Strawn got shot down today on a 128-plane raid. Big soft ball series on in squadron.

April 29ᵗʰ . . .
New pilots came in today; we need them.

May 6ᵗʰ 1943 . . .
Bizerta fell to U.S. today, Tunis to 8ᵗʰ Army.

May 10ᵗʰ ...
Eddie Rickenbacker was here today. Heard Lt. Strawn is in Tunis.

May 16ᵗʰ ...
Drove to Korba on Cape Bon today in jeep with Ralph Apple.

May 17ᵗʰ ...
Abandoned German and Italian equipment here at Korba. Many of the guys are commandeering operating motorcycles here now. There is so much equipment and armaments about. Nobody is in charge yet.

Apple and I were coming back from detonating some hand grenades we found in a quarry and saw two German soldiers sleeping or hiding in a corn field. We didn't have our Tommy guns with us so we used a couple of jammed rifles we had picked up and marched them down through our bivouac area to Ops. It was an unexpected sight for our guys to see. Went swimming later in ocean ... big rip tides off Korba.

May 19ᵗʰ ...
Went shooting with German Mauser I took from prisoner. Found some Italian coins.

May 26ᵗʰ ...
Wind blew very hard today, dust and sand everywhere. Mess hall was a real mess ... sand in food.

June 2ⁿᵈ 1943 ...
Went to see Churchill, Eden and Montgomery today for pep talk.

June 4th ...

Another bad dirt storm today. We're in the desert and must expect this sort of thing. We'll be moving out soon, I guess.

June 5th ...

We'll be leaving here tomorrow for assembly for the move on Sicily. To go near Algiers area for a while. Spent the day packing up equipment, supplies, personal belongings, etc. We filled in all the slit trenches outside our pup tents. We leave in the morning.

June 6th ...

At dawn today we were awakened by a strafing run of *ME-109*s and *FW-190*s on our bivouac and dispersal areas. Apple and I had our pup tents together. I got hit in the left hip on the first pass. Not only did we not have enough time to run anywhere, we had filled in our trenches the night before. *Jerry* must have known we were going to move today.

Everyone who could run, did, and things were pretty hectic for a few minutes. I managed to get to the Medic tent, not really knowing how bad I was hit — we were so excited. About then, someone yelled, "... Here they come again." I just lay down on my back and watched them make another run. I guess it's better to run or hide but if you can't, it's a terrifying experience to watch them come down dropping fragmentation bombs and shooting their wing guns. One of the "frag" bombs missed our tent by four feet and put 52 holes in the tent and one into me.

An attack like that is to maim, not kill. If maimed, now someone has to take care of the wounded and he's out of service for awhile.

They only made two passes as a few of our operational

42

ack-ack guns fired at them. By the time we scrambled a few *Spits*, the Germans were probably landing somewhere in Sicily. Seven or eight of us got hit, no one real bad, and off we went to a British field hospital. The squadron went on with their plans for the day. I'll be away from them for a spell.

NOTE:
As sometimes happens, funny stories can come out of a panic situation like that morning at Korba, Tunisia.

First, that manner of awakening is about the rudest way one can imagine. There's the din of explosions and machine gun fire and racing airplane engines, rancid smoke and dust, and the ground shocks. All of that together at one time brings one's adrenalin forward for instant use. In a second, under those conditions, a person evaluates first, that he's alive and well (or he isn't) and that his best chance of continued survival is to remove ones self from this point of danger. We were convinced at that moment we were in a point of danger. Since we could not get below ground surface, running seemed our best defense.

Now, adjoining our bivouac area was a standing cornfield, one cared for dutifully by some Arabs. Since that was close and would afford shelter, Nolan Mann said he decided to run into this cornfield before the next strafing pass. However, he was so excited and running so fast, he said, " . . . . . I ran completely through this cornfield and out the other side into the open before I even realized I was into corn . . . . ." It was quite an experience, one that I didn't get to share with the guys until I rejoined the squadron two months later in Sicily.

July 10ᵗʰ . . .
Big Invasion Day, today.

43

July 12th . . .

This British field hospital is a Nissen Hut like what we were billeted in in Chichester, England. Most of the guys I see aren't hurt too bad. No one seems to be in any kind of a hurry here ... like there's a war going on out there and we're needed. If they don't decide to remove the shrapnel from my hip, I hope they let me go back to the Squadron now in Sicily.

An amusing thing one of the medics here is a captured German. He speaks some English and lets you know they are a super race, and anyone not performing like Hitler, should be removed and not be a burden on their society.

July 20th . . .

X-rays have convinced them the incision to remove the metal from my hip might be worse than leaving the shrapnel in for now. So I can plan to go back after the paperwork is processed.

July 24th . . .

I got some G.I. clothes today for return to the Squadron.

August 5th 1943. . .

I joined up with my squadron today after recuperating in an English field hospital near Algiers. It was quite a trick getting back by an open 40 & 8 flat car on a French-run train, British lorries, a boat ride, and so forth. We're at a metal strip on the Tyrrhenian Sea in Sicily.

August 7th . . .

Went swimming before daylight today. Apple and I go out far and float.

August 9th . . .
One of our pilots brought in an Italian *Macchi* plane today.

August 13th . . .
Made Sergeant today!

August 16th . . .
Sicilian campaign over today.

August 19th . . .
Mann, Bain and I visited Palermo today on a lumber detail.

August 20th . . .
General Henri Giraud (Commander of Free French forces) landed today at Termini. I saw him walking on the beach from my cot in the vineyard where we are living now.

August 23rd . . .
Saw two in a *Spitfire* for the first time today.

August 25th . . .
*P-38*s made a big raid today, some landed at our field on the way back to their field. Some needed fuel.

August 26th . . .
General Patton visited here today. We were to shape up a bit for his visit. Some of us disappeared in the grape vineyard where we are bivouacked now.

August 30th . . .
It rained today and we got miserably wet. My cot is in this vineyard and doesn't have much protection over it.

August 31ˢᵗ ...
An Italian transport landed here today for negotiations.

September 4ᵗʰ 1943 ...
Left today for Milazzo.

September 7ᵗʰ ...
Italy is invaded today. Lots of missions.

September 9ᵗʰ ...
We go swimming whenever the planes are out since we're
so near the sea (Tyrrhenian.) Our runway is practically on the
beach.

September 16ᵗʰ ...
Milton Clark (a boyhood friend who was eventually the
Best Man at our wedding) flew in today in one of his *P-40*s.
They're supporting the invasion also.

September 20ᵗʰ ....
An Italian plane landed at Milazzo today and gave up.

September 21ˢᵗ ...
Left today at 2:00 p.m. for Italy. Flew around Etna, and
landed at Catania, then to Italy.

September 22ⁿᵈ ...
Had a close one this morning as we were coming back
from breakfast at our field kitchen. The Germans were
strafing the road we were walking back on to the barracks.
The bullets went down the right ditch and, luckily, Apple and
I dove into the left ditch, and prayed a little. It was over before
we realized what was happening.

September 23rd . . .
Living in these barracks now isn't bad. We have the mess hall downstairs, a nice setup. We installed a sink in the room we're in and I'm trying to get an Italian radio going that I found.

September 26th . . .
Milton Clark flew in to see me again. He made Captain recently. I hung onto the cockpit and wing as he taxied out to take off, then I jumped off. I'll see him back in the States, I hope.

September 27th . . .
Drove down to the docks today and sent in an application for a Social Psychology course from Penn State. We're now south of Salerno at Monte Corvino where we had a few restless nights as we followed the landing troops, almost too closely. The Navy was supporting the coast landings to the north and we were told not to bed down in any gullies that ran east and west because that's where the Navy shells were landing. I saw my first battered American tank burning with the bodies still inside. Sobering. The Germans were still in the hills and landing their 88 m.m. shells on our troops. But we prevailed.

October 12th 1943 . . .
At 9:00 a.m. this forenoon, seven of us moved by truck from Monte Corvino airdrome south of Salerno (where the first landings were made) to an airfield, Pomigliano by name, about six miles northeast of Naples. We came through the new city of Pompeii, the old Pompeii being covered by lava when Vesuvius erupted in 79 A.D. We didn't get to see much so we intend to return soon.

About 1:30 p.m., Bain and I returned to Naples from the airfield to see what the city was like. We weren't there long but I did get my sister a pair of leather gloves that I'll send home at Christmas time. Got back to barracks at 4:00 p.m. We are to live in evacuated Italian workers' apartments. Five of us are in a room, viz: Bain, Mann, Pankratz, Apple and myself. Very nice room, bathroom close. When I washed this morning, I looked out the window and saw Mt. Vesuvius smoking. It smokes most of the time.

October 13th ...
Left this forenoon and went to Pompeii (Bain and I.) We hired a guide (fifty cents) and toured the entire ancient city. Saw and took pictures of the amphitheater, temple of Apollo, Civil Forum. Also saw the Stabian Baths and the Frigidarium of Women (ladies' bath) and the house of the balcony. Much of this town has been restored to its original form. It was built before Christ. I bought a book on Pompeii and also got a piece of mosaic marble from the wall of an old wine shop.

Just went outside to fill my canteen from the water trailer and noticed flames coming from the top of Vesuvius. Guess I'll go to bed now though it's only 8:30 p.m.

October 14th ...
Ellsworth Minor, Savage, Bain, Apple and I laid some telephone lines this morning from the drome to our barracks, by a blown-up Macchi engine plant. The Germans blew it up when they left, the most thorough job of demolition I've seen yet. There were smaller shell craters, signs the Allies had helped them previously. I understand they rebuilt and reconditioned engines here for the Italian fighter plane, the *Macchi*.

It rained in the p.m. so I read a *Downbeat* magazine and wrote a letter home. We played Casino tonight until 9:00 p.m.

October 15th . . .

I worked on our radio this forenoon. Found some loose wires but still it doesn't work right. May have to take it to a repair shop where they have a circuit analyzer, etc. We don't have the right equipment in our radio shop. Today, I looked over the remains of some six engine *(ME-232)* planes that the Germans burned before they left They certainly are big things.

Harned Bain, Larmon Powell and I had our picture taken by a street photographer.

To me it's a pitiful sight to see the way these little kids here grab for the food scraps before we throw them into the garbage cans. I never saw anything like it. They must be starving, or maybe they just want a different diet. The people here emphasize destitution and look for gifts, favors, etc. I guess it's a way of life ... they take what comes.

October 19th . . .

Bain and I hitch-hiked to Naples this morning from the airdrome at Pomigliano. We went in about 8:00 a.m. and came back at 3:00 p.m. We had both decided we wanted to spend the day there, see what we could and then forget it. As many of the sights are closed for the duration, we didn't see much. Of course we could see the street statues (Garibaldi and others) that are so numerous in Naples, their fine buildings (from the architectural standpoint,) Via Roma Street, etc.

We each bought a small throw rug for by our beds in an Italian five and dime store. In another store I bought a small chrome effigy of a golfer for fifty lire. The salesman said the price was 100 lire ($1.00.) I said I'd give 50 lire, and he said, "Sold!"

As it was in England, Africa and Sicily, it is in Italy ... these people know they can get just about what they want from us Yanks. I guess they're right ... we're suckers. I also bought some picture postcards.

We visited the newly renovated *Red Cross Club* which is O.K.. I talked to Lucky Martin, the famous *Red Cross Club* organizer. I've read of his exploits. We walked around some more, were accosted a number of times, observed the standard of living of these people, played three games of 8-ball (my first since the States) and started back to the barracks.

I understand from lectures by Italian Chaplains that it is the character of the people of Naples and vicinity to be satisfied with little or nothing, the working class anyway. Apparently their code of living is, "get along on the least." Anyway, they live in filth and corruption, wash their clothes in the water in the gutters, allowing their children to urinate there, etc. They eat little and go about barefooted, women and men alike.

We saw this sort of thing in North Africa. Had I come directly here from the U.S., I would have been shocked and bewildered no end, but being in Africa first, I'm more or less inoculated to this kind of stuff. I don't think the war alone brought this way of living on. I'll bet it's been going on for a long time. Maybe Fascism caused it. I now know why so many Italians immigrate to the States. I would, too.

October 20th ...

I didn't do much today, just the usual line work. However, in the evening three of us went to an Italian family's home. A lot of the fellows do this but it was my first experience since England. This particular home was very plain but not destitute or dirty. There was the usual large family ... four girls and three boys. We gave them some cigarettes and biscuits for which they were thankful and, they in return, gave us some wine. We didn't drink much as we didn't like it that much. We gesticulated and talked for a while, and I found one of the boys was an artist. There seems to be a number of them in Italy. He does portrait work, so I made a date to have mine done at 9:00 a.m. on the 22nd. Hope it is good ... I'll send it home. When we left they did the usual hand-shaking (women, too) and cheek-kissing. This is an old Italian tradition, to kiss one's cheek or hand to show appreciation. All these people seem very friendly and it is evident they are glad we are here, and the war is over for them. Of course, their traditionally high appraisal of the States helps us, too. Got to bed at 10:00 p.m. KP for me tomorrow.

October 22nd ...

Today I went to the home of the so-called artist to have him make a portrait of me. He made a pencil sketch and I didn't like it (no resemblance) so he is making an oil one now. It will take a few days, I guess. I don't think he is one of the best over here; I'll see how he does. Bought a bunch of walnuts today. There seems to be many of these fruit cart dealers along the streets. They have for sale apples, grapes, lemons, persimmons, walnuts and hazelnuts. We were raided last night, not the airdrome but close enough to put us on our toes. They raided the harbor and outlying districts, I think.

October 23rd ...

Still sitting for the portrait and eating walnuts. It was a nice fall day today. Fall seems to have a certain tang to it that I like. Reminds me of hunting season back home. They are harvesting small corn fields here now. We were raided again last night. *Jerry* must have an important target.

October 24th ...
Sat again for the portrait today. Got an idea on how to fix up an old phonograph one of the boys, Jerry Pankratz has, so it will play through our radio when it gets fixed up.

Went to the show, *Star Spangled Rhythm*, tonight and half way through we were raided again (somewhat closer tonight) and didn't see any more of it. Listened to a football game between Michigan and Minnesota when we got back to the barracks. Michigan won 49 to 6. To bed at 10:30 p.m.

October 25th ...
Another nice fall day. Still eating walnuts and apples. Today we bought an electric pickup for the old phonograph and got the radio out of the repair shop. The radio works swell and with the record player plugged into it, it works just as well. It has swell tone, especially the bass, it comes out swell. Hope I get the records from home I asked for. Sat for the portrait again today for about 20 minutes. Was on guard at the drome from 10:00 p.m. to 2:00 a.m.

October 26th ...
We worked on our radio more today and got it working O.K. again. Playing records through it really works wizard. Saw a very rugged plane crash today. A *P-51* landing without flaps bounced when he hit the runway and skidded through the dispersal area damaging the wing of one *Spitfire*, and completely wiping out three others besides ruining the *P-51*. No one, including the pilot, was harmed ... a miracle. I never saw so much damage done by one plane in such a short time.

Sat one hour and forty-five minutes for portrait again

today. Took an old pocket watch I bought in Africa out to be fixed tonight. It needs a crystal and adjusting. Hope it can be fixed. Was on guard four hours in the middle of the night last night. Better go to bed now at 7:00 p.m.

October 27th ...
I received word today I am eligible for non-resident study at Penn State College now, and for resident work post-war. Received word from Mom today saying they received part of the packages I sent from Sicily. I bought them in Palermo. Very glad to hear this.
Today three G.I. trucks of us went on a very interesting tour. Our learned Chaplain, Father Kuzma, went along as guide and told us much. We started at 9:00 a.m. and first went to Mt. Vesuvious. There is a railway track that runs from the bottom nearly to the top, but it hasn't been running for a month or so now, so we rode up a very narrow and winding road in the trucks. A three-months-ago eruption covered part of the road so we had to walk about a mile to get to the very top. The top of the mountain is comparatively level and, of course, is hardened lava. In about the center on top of this lava is the cone of the crater. It has been formed in the last year by the ash that is constantly blown from the crater's depths. It is approximately 300 feet high.

Although it isn't exactly advisable, we climbed to the rim of the crater, took some pictures of the inside and escaped without getting hit by the 2000 degree F. chunks of lava that are coming out at regular intervals. When it is about to be blown out, there is a smothered explosion and everyone ducks. A sulphur-smelling smoke hovers around the rim and makes it very difficult to breathe. At the bottom of this ash cone, out of the range of the flying stuff, are the lava ovens. It is here that the lava bubbles up from the depths in different places. Attendants are only too willing to make an ash tray or sink a coin in this 2000 degree stuff for 10 lire. I bought a couple. We ate our dinner here, took some pictures and walked and ran back to the trucks.

There is a very beautiful view of the winding road, Naples and the harbor from up on Vesuvius. Our Chaplain told us the Italians sometimes call it Vesuvio (feminine for Vesuvius) because no one has ever been on it. Of course, that's incorrect as I was on it myself. They must mean no one has ever been "in her."

From there, we went down the hill, bought some cards enroute and on to Herculaneum, one of the three cities that was covered by Vesuvius when it erupted in 79 A.D. It is similar to Pompeii and is outstanding for its fine mosaic marble floors, (I got a piece from a room unusual for this,) walls and ceilings. A peculiar feature about the excavation of Herculaneum is that it was paid for by the late John D. Rockefeller ... beating the income tax apparently. I bought some cards of the place and we then went to the new Pompeii to see the beautiful cathedral there, built also by John D. I was very much impressed with the bright color of the interior of this great building. I understand it is the world's third best ... St. Peters in Rome first, Westminster Abbey in London, second. I may be able to say I saw them all some day soon.

After this, we went back to our barracks at Pomigliano Airdrome much satisfied with the day's trip and much tired. When I got back to the room, the boys had connected up the radio and I had three letters and two *Time Magazines* there. To bed, tired, at 7:30 p.m.

October 28ᵗʰ ...
I went down today to get the portrait I have been sitting

for. It was finished, but isn't so hot. I had a couple pencil sketches made that aren't as bad as the painting. As long as I spent so much time sitting for it, I guess I might as well send it home, but I know my folks won't like it. I gave him $1.50 for his work. Anyway, I can say I had my portrait painted in Naples, Italy, if that's anything.

For supper tonight we had turkey, mashed potatoes, gravy, cranberry sauce, fruit cocktail, bread and hot cocoa. A step from the usual line of food we get. Very good. I got a phonograph arm and pickup from an English lieutenant. If I can obtain a motor somewhere I'll construct a phonograph to play through our radio. To bed at 8:30 p.m.

November 1st 1943 ...

I sent the lava souvenirs, postcards, etc. home today. I hope they don't get lost enroute. Nice fall day today, typical of fall back home. I'd like to be there hunting today ... today's the first day of rabbit season. I hope someone takes Bob (my beagle hound) out so he gets some exercise.

Some of the boys are getting passes to the Isle of Capri, which lies about 25 miles off Naples. I understand the cost of such a trip is somewhat excessive so I don't plan to go. It's just more or less a resort place, I guess.

We (the Naples area) got raided again last night. Heard the planes buzzing overhead, low.

November 8th ...

A year ago today we were landing in North Africa. The Allies have done a lot in the last year. Hope another year sees as much more. Rained today so we were released for most of the day. I went down at 4:00 p.m. to meet four planes when they came back from convoy patrol near Naples. It was real cool as the sun went down. Typically fall, I love it. Makes me think of home and hunting season. Just finished sewing a wool blanket on either side of my comforter. Should make a very warm combination. Can still zip it open and shut. Imagine I'll need something warm for this coming winter ... might be outside occasionally.

I may go to the Isle of Capri tomorrow. It's a few miles off Naples and a boat leaves about 9:00 in the morning. I'd like to go there for a few hours. Get a little souvenir maybe.

November 9th ...

We went to Naples this morning at 9:00 a.m. and down to the docks to catch a boat for the Isle of Capri, and found one wasn't going until 1:00 p.m. As I was sort of unlucky last month in a poker game, I decided not to go. We would have to stay all night and that takes much money, I understand. So I decided to go back into Naples. I walked around some here, bought a wooden cigarette case and decided to bum around some.

It was about 10:00 a.m. when I started. I caught an English truck first and rode southeast about 20 miles to a town of Castellmare, a little town south of Naples opposite the Isle of Capri. I didn't stay long, catching another English truck (driven by some Indians) and I rode to Pompeii. I went to the famous cathedral again and got a little pamphlet this time. This surely is a beautiful place. While in Pompeii I bought a couple little boxes with inlaid designs on the tops. Also a cigarette case.

I caught an American truck from Pompeii back to Naples and another to the airdrome. Got back about 3:30 p.m. It was such a nice fall day that I enjoyed the trip very much. Got my first Christmas box from home today.

November 10th ...

Got raided at 3:30 a.m. this morning. They'll have to quit getting us up at that time.

November 12th ...

Read quite a bit of the book, *Mission To Moscow*, I got from home. I also decided today to make me a foot locker from some of the sheet aluminum that is in some of these blown-up factories. I'll try living out of a foot locker instead of a barracks bag for a while.

Eighteen *FW-190*'s and *ME-109*'s raided our airdrome this morning. They dropped only a few bombs and strafed a little ... little damage. I was in our operations building when I heard them diving. Needless to say I got to an air-raid tunnel in a hurry. Today I got the gym shoes from home that I sent for sometime ago. They are O.K..

November 16th ...

Today I received a couple Christmas boxes from Mom. Cookies, nuts, dictionary, books, white ski cap, etc. I might get in trouble wearing the white ski cap so I decided to send it out with our laundry lady to get it dyed brown. I started work on my foot locker today. I dug some sheet aluminum from under the debris of one of the blown-up buildings.

November 17th ...

It rained all day today so we were released. I worked on my foot locker. It should be O.K. when I get it finished.

November 18th ...

Took the first shower today since La Senia ... one year ago!

November 19ᵗʰ ...

Worked on the foot locker today, about finished it.

November 23ʳᵈ ...

It rained again today so I finished my foot locker. I put my clothes, et cetera, in it tonight. Surely is wizard!

November 27ᵗʰ ...

Made a clothes rack from some aluminum tubing today. I brought it over on the truck when we came home tonight. Everybody laughed at how funny it looked but it surely works nice in the room ... something different. I fastened it together with bolts so I can take it apart when we leave and reassemble it elsewhere. I plan to make a stand to hold my helmet (wash stand) on the same order.

December 2ⁿᵈ 1943 ...

Much air activity today. First I've seen for quite some time. I guess we've got it if we need it. I got three birthday cards today.

December 3ʳᵈ ...

Guess I'm 24 today. Ellsworth Minor and Carl Scott had birthdays today, too. More activity today. Took a shower tonight.

December 5ᵗʰ ...

Our squadron had a dance tonight so we were released early this afternoon. We took a shower and got our blouses back from the pressers. There was a show on for our group, *Stage Door Canteen*, so we went to it before the dance. Got to the dance about 8:30 p.m. Most of the fellows were there. There were Italian girls and some Red Cross girls. I danced with a R. C. girl, the first time I've danced in over fourteen months. I hope I don't go another fourteen without dancing. The boys were all happy and Ralph Apple and I got a lot of laughs just watching them. We listened to the band all night long. After intermission and the sandwiches, the Italian girls left. These people disgust me, but I guess they are hungry.

December 7th ...

Got up early this morning for an early mission. As we were calling in the ships an English *Mosquito* came in from a night mission. It makes a guy feel funny to see them flying around in the early light knowing they have been out, maybe as far north as Milan, shooting up trains, etc. The English *Beaufighter* and *Mosquito* have certainly proved their mettle. I inquired at the Air Transport Office about getting a ride over to see Milton Clark. Can be arranged, I guess.

December 11th ...

I got some records from home today ... four out of six were broken. We have about fifteen records for our record player now. We really have a nice set-up here. Five of us in the room and we get along swell. We got a couple 100-watt light bulbs so we have plenty of light to read and play bridge by at night. We go to bed about 10:00 p.m. each evening and get up shortly after 6:00 a.m. in the morning. Our mess hall, bar, supply and orderly rooms are downstairs so everything is convenient enough. Considering everything, it is better than La Senia in Africa. Trucks take us to the line.

December 16th ...

"Ike" Eisenhower, Gen. Mark Clark and Gen. Jimmy Doolittle flew in today in a *Fortress*.

December 20th ...

I see my name is on the bulletin board to be at a formation tomorrow at 3:30 p.m. to get the Purple Heart.

December 21st ...

Today the Colonel of our Group pinned the Purple Heart on seven of us and congratulated us all. He told us he didn't want us to get oak leaf clusters for them.

December 22nd ...

Was on KP duty today and guard at night.

December 25th ...

Today, Christmas, we were released from the line in the p.m. We popped some corn that one of the fellows in the room had gotten in a package from home and at 5:00 p.m. we ate a big supper ... turkey, ice cream, etc. I opened a couple packages today I had received but hadn't opened.

December 28th ...

Surely was a lot of flying today. A B-26 came in on one engine and cracked up. I saw the first *Fortress* I've seen with a chin turret.

Chapter Three
1944

January 1ˢᵗ 1944 ...

The beginning of another working year. I wonder if this year will see the finish of part of it. I think so. Our squadron had a dance tonight and I went. Quite a large number of Italian girls came out from Naples, sort of nice of them. I danced most of the evening with what I considered a very attractive girl. She couldn't dance so well but she was cute. I also danced with another girl who was the smoothest dancer I've seen since the States. We got along swell and I was flattered when she chose not to be tagged by some other soldiers. I really enjoyed it all.

January 3ʳᵈ ...

Well, the rumor now is that we are to be going on another invasion sometime in the near future. No details yet. May go east, eh? I don't know what I'll do with my foot locker ... maybe make a box for it. The Red Cross girls were around with doughnuts again tonight. (Our shower here is a godsend.) We'll miss them when we leave. Although we have it very convenient here, now that there is a move approaching, I'm ready to go. Might as well see more country. We'll be seeing it the hard way, that's the only thing.

January 5ᵗʰ ...

The Appenine Mountains we see in a northeasterly direction from here are beautiful with snow on them,. Especially when the sun sets. I don't imagine the soldiers fighting on them appreciate it like we do. Mt. Vesuvio this morning has snow on her almost to the bottom. The first for quite a few years, I heard. Naples is out of bounds now to all transient troops ... an epidemic of Typhus they say. The talk is that it is due to a venereal outbreak as much as anything. We were shown the government show, *Sex Hygiene*, a few days ago. It impressed me even if it didn't anyone else. The morals of these girls over here have hit rock bottom. I never even surmised anything like it existed. Guess I'll go down on the street and get one of the many shoe shiners to shine my gym shoes.

January 9ᵗʰ ...

Today, very unexpectedly, I went up in a *Beaufighter*, the famous English patrol plane. Some are stationed at this field and as they go up each afternoon to check them out, they will let anybody go up with them that wishes. I got one of our pilot's chutes and went along. I stood up behind the pilot (a Sergeant) and watched the controls, gauges, etc. It was lots of fun. We went up to about 3500 feet, and cruised along at 220 mph most of the time. I'd like to go up again and take along a head set so I could hear what goes on.

Today also for the first time, I "ran up" a *Spitfire* and drove a 6 by 6 G.I. truck. More fun and new experiences today. Tonight, I'm on guard.

January 11ᵗʰ ...

Today was my day off. As I read some of my magazines,

I was amused to hear the Italian janitors out in the halls singing songs that have the same melody as ours only in a different language. A couple were *The Woodpecker Song* and *O Solo Mio*, the latter being an Italian one.

Today I got my first text book from Penn State, *Experimental Social Psychology* by Murphy and Newcome. As soon as I get the other one I can start sending answer sheets back.

I heard today we are to have another Squadron dance the 17th of this month. Good.

January 15th ...

It's definite now that we are leaving for another field soon. I sort of dislike leaving this place with the showers, show, barracks, Naples close by, etc. Went to a show tonight. Went to one last night, too. We're high live-ers now ...

January 17th ...

Today a few fellows left for the other field. The rest of us are to leave tomorrow. It seemed funny tonight in the room with Harned Bain gone. It's always that way when someone is gone. I wonder what we'll do when we get back in civilian life and there isn't much excitement? We just sat around and read tonight, all of us sort of regretful of leaving such a nice set-up. We have been here the longest of anywhere, three months and six days. This has been a very enjoyable and seemingly short stay. I'll bet where we go we'll know we're back in the war ... back into tents for one thing sure.

January 18th ...

Today at 9:30 a.m., six of us left on a G.I. truck for the other field. We went through Naples, Santa Maria, Capua and Castle Volturno. The field is a very plain one compared to the last one. The runway is of steel matting and our bivouac area is about a mile from the field. On the way up we saw some *P-47*'s and some very large gas dumps and tank farms. Bain had a pyramidal tent set up for us. There is to be six in a tent, I guess. We didn't get a stove made today and I about froze at night.

January 19th ...

We went down to the field today and set up the radio-shop tent. There isn't much to the field. We made a stove of gas cans today and wired for electric lights and radio. The stove is a wizard thing. I slept a little warmer at night. Think I'll try to draw some handle bar jobs to sleep in.

January 20th ...

We decided to let our 130-octane fire burn all night so I slept fairly well. I still have a few adjustments to make though before I will get the most comfort from my sack. Maybe I should put more blankets underneath me. Since I sold my air mattress for $20, cold air comes up through the bottom, I think.

January 21st ...

I drew some long johns underwear today so I should sleep better tonight. In the tent tonight we did a very unusual thing for soldiers in the field to do ... we made some fudge. A couple of us had a vague memory of the procedure. We used a cup of sugar, some peanuts, condensed milk and vanilla extract tablets. Peculiarly, it turned out very good. May do it again. Tonight we were told our forces are to strike up the coast tomorrow morning at 1:00 a.m. about 25 miles south of Rome. We may go there if an airfield is captured. I certainly hope they make this thing good, it may shorten the war.

January 22nd ...

Today I was on KP. I guess the Rangers and Commandos got ashore with little trouble south of Rome. There were many missions flown today. Our Squadron had the first mission over the battle area, no opposition.

On a mission at dusk our Group C.O. flying one of our planes, shot down a *M.E. 109* and our Squadron C.O. damaged an *F.W. 190.* We played cards tonight. Our tent is pretty O.K. with the stove, lights and radio. I still have my foot locker and clothes rack, very valuable both of them.

January 24th ...

Naples is open for us again. Must be they have the Typhus epidemic under control. I might go in on my day off. I haven't been in for quite some time. We made another batch of fudge tonight. Turned out O.K. again.

January 28th ...

Tonight Jerry Pankratz and Leroy Marsh, both from the tent and from the radio section, left with another squadron for the beach head, Anzio, south of Rome. I don't think the rest of us will go very soon.

February 1st 1944 ...

Today Bain and I hitchhiked around a bit. We bummed back to Caserta, where the 5th Army Headquarters is. The building is an enormous thing. It was previously a king's palace. It is reputed to have three thousand rooms. We saw a couple of W.A.A.C.'s there, and started back. Stopped at Capua and saw a bridge the Engineers built across the Volturno River ... a masterpiece, I think. I rode back from there with our executive officer. Got back in time for supper. Had a cup of coffee and to bed at 9:00 p.m.

February 2ⁿᵈ ...

Some of the fellows caught a few Italians in the area tonight with cigarettes they had stolen from some of our tents. They took them away to the Provost Marshall. Some of these Italians are not much good, to my idea.

February 7ᵗʰ ...

Today Norman Rieck, Bain and I went to Naples. We went in at 8:30 a.m. and came back at 7:30 in the evening. While there, we went to a show, saw a good jam session at the *Red Cross Club*, and bought some gadgets. The *Red Cross Club* is quite nice now. We had some cakes and coffee in the snack bar, played some records in the music room and rested in some over-stuffed chairs. Saw some W.A.A.C.'s too. Har Har.

February 13ᵗʰ ...

Today I went to Naples again. Rieck and I went to a show, ate at the snack bar ... had some ice cream, and very good it was ... watched a jazz session in the lounge and joined the *Red Cross Club*. I bought a coral necklace for my sister. I asked the salesman how much it was; he said $1.50. I said I'd give him $1 and a pack of cigarettes. He wrapped it up. Good cigarettes are at a premium here. I think the next time I go in I'll take some and trade them for things.

February 17ᵗʰ ...

Went in town today, Bain and I. I traded two cartons of cigarettes at different stores for coral bracelets, necklaces, etc. Saw a show, watched a jam session and came back at 5:00 p.m.

February 24ᵗʰ ...

Bain and I went to Naples again today. Were accosted several times. Went to a show and did the usual things.

March 1st 1944 ...

It is rainy today so I decided not to go to Naples again, my day off. I finished my third Psychology lesson and prepared it for sending.

March 5th ...

Heard the rumor today we are to get different airplanes, *P-51's, Mustangs*. I hate to part with our *Spitfires*. They are a great little plane with one of the best reputations. I imagine when we get them we will have a change in our operations. May go to strategical work instead of tactical.

March 8th ...

Went to Naples for the day today. Show, etc. My day off.

March 10th ...

Well, we got the first two *Mustangs* today. *P-51 B's*, the latest I guess. Four bladed props and boucoupe gasoline in the wings. One of the best fighter planes the States makes, it's rumored.

March 12th ...

We were sold three bottles of Coca Cola today in our rations. This war is certainly becoming streamlined. I can well remember when we first landed in England, scarcely anything like this was available. Not even American cigarettes ... no American candy, fruit, food or anything. Those first three or four months there were sort of rough in that respect. I didn't smoke that much so that part didn't bother me. Some of the boys that did, found the English cigarettes sort of bad to take, what there were to get. Now that we have the shipping problem under control, more things are obtainable. We got wool flying boots and jackets a few days ago, something that would have come in very handy at Oran, Africa. We about froze from exposure working our way east in Africa that winter.

March 14ᵗʰ ...

I went to Naples again today. I didn't go to a show as usual but instead in the forenoon I walked down to the docks to the Aquarium. I guess it isn't as complete as it was pre-war (the Germans threw the octopus into the street) but I still enjoyed it. I had never visited one before. Saw coral, starfish, sea horses, lobsters, fish, etc. In the afternoon I watched some basketball games, enjoyed that, too. Came back at 5:00 p.m.

March 25ᵗʰ ...

Today I got back from a 5-day stay on the Isle of Capri. It was my turn to go so I left last Monday. It is about a two-hour boat ride off Naples. When we got there, three of us, Bob Wetzel, Joe Lankford and myself, registered at a peace-time hotel that has been commandeered by the U.S. Army Air Forces. We had a nice three-man room with a southern view facing the sea ... nice thick mattresses on the beds.

Tuesday we went scouting around. Went to both *Red Cross Clubs*. The largest *Red Cross Club* is a large villa and really nice. In the p.m. we got our rations at the PX. Wednesday we went out in a row boat to the Blue Grotto. This is an under-ground cavern which is reputed to be something beautiful. I didn't think it was worth the 65 cents it cost to see it. In the afternoon we went cruising around the island in a long-hooded touring car we rented, a dollar each for about an hour. We went up to Ana Capri and Piccola Marina. I took a few pictures.

Thursday it rained and we sat around and read, played Ping Pong, etc. Friday, I bought some post cards, a capri bell, and shopped around some. We walked up a steep hill south of the hotel and got a good view of Capri, the Villas, the sea, etc. We went to a dance at night. I danced some but there was too much tagging for me.

Saturday we got up at 6:00 a.m. and caught the boat back at 8:00 a.m., and got to Naples at 10:00 a.m.. Got back to camp at 2:30 p.m., the end of a nice trip. I didn't need the rest but it was very nice to go somewhere away from the idea of work, and have someone else make your bed, serve your meals, etc. One of the nice things about it was the absence of guns firing and gasoline engines running. I was strictly at ease over there and think it was very much worth the $15 I spent. I'd go again the first chance I got.

March 27ᵗʰ ...

Old Vesuvio is calming down now. Ash is still billowing up from its depths but the lava has ceased to flow. For about a week all hell broke loose inside her. When we were at Capri, the ash came down like snow, 25 miles away, too. The town near her really got a beating ... people killed, etc.

March 28ᵗʰ ...

We've been working quite sedulously lately, getting the new *P-51*'s in flying condition. Today we finished the radio part of it. The late ones are coming through unpainted. They look like peace time jobs. I guess they will be O.K. after we get used to them. Right now they seem much different than the *Spit*, more complicated ... an American trait.

March 30ᵗʰ ...

Today most of our good old *Spitfires* left. Sort of hated to see them go. It seemed like the 31ˢᵗ and *Spitfires* were something to go together. I guess the latest *Mustang* is quite a ship, too. Today we were told we are to leave for another field tomorrow ... one over by Foggia, I guess. Miles from no where, I'll bet.

April 3rd 1944 ...

Some of the trucks came today to move our equipment and us to a new field, one over by Foggia. We loaded most of the equipment and plan to leave tomorrow.

April 4th ...

Today at 12:30 p.m. we left for Foggia, about a hundred miles from Castel Volturno. It was a long, dusty ride, very scenic though. Went across the Appenine's. Saw many destitute towns and villages. It certainly is a pity the way these people have to live. The towns are dirtier and smell worse than the Arab towns ... we thought they were the worst possible. We got to the new camp at about 9:00 p.m. Our bivouac area is about seven and a half miles from the Air Drome, seems like quite a ways. We are to be in buildings if we want to, or we may move into a tent for more privacy. We slept in a building tonight, all the radio men.

April 5th ...

All the radio men are going to move into tents, I guess. There seems to be a lot of buildings here for mess halls, orderly rooms, day rooms, etc.

We went down to the drome this afternoon. It's a pretty big field, quite a long runway. All kinds of planes stationed here ... a reconnaissance group is here with British *Mosquitos, Spit X1's, Fortresses, Liberators, P-38's,* etc. Our Squadron is the only one of the group that has its full quota of *Mustangs.* We should be operating in a few weeks. I guess the heavies are very eager to have our planes go along with them.

70

April 8ᵗʰ ...

It gets sort of tiresome riding to the line and back four times a day, very dusty. I guess this post won't be so bad when they get it fixed up. We are to have a camp laundry, PX, nice Day Room, mess hall, shows at least three times a week, etc. We have a soft ball diamond close to our bivouac area. We have been having sectional games nights after work.

April 12ᵗʰ ...

All three squadrons are fully outfitted with new *Mustangs* now. Most of them are silver, as are the *B-17*'s, *24*'s, *38*'s, and many other American planes now. We are to escort heavy bombers over Yugoslavia, Rumania, Hungary, France, and wherever else it's necessary for our bombers to go.

April 15ᵗʰ ...

Tomorrow our pilots are to go on their first escort mission with heavy bombers. Sixteen planes from each Squadron, I think.

April 16ᵗʰ ...

Today our planes took off at 9:00 a.m. and escorted *B-17*'s on a bombing mission to Rumania. They bombed a town, Turno Severin. We lost one pilot over Yugoslavia, shot down by a *B-17* gunner. Those gunners don't take any chances, it seems. There was no air opposition but plenty of flak. Another mission again tomorrow at 9:30 a.m. Up again in the morning at 5:30 a.m., I suppose.

April 17ᵗʰ ...

Today our pilots went with more heavies on a raid to Sofia, Bulgaria. The Colonel of our group, flying with our Squadron, got two confirmed; a Captain got one and a probable one, and another pilot got two probables. We lost one pilot again today, no one knows what happened to him. Another mission tomorrow. Busy, eh?

April 20th ...

Harned Bain and I decided today we should build a shower as the Squadron doesn't have one now. If we could get a nice one built, we might charge a slight fee. Our planes went to Trieste today with more heavies.

April 21st ...

Today our planes went to Ploesti, Rumania. Quite a trip. Weather kept the heavy bombers from bombing the targets, marshaling yards. Harned and I worked on our shower some today. I've been thinking on it since we got the idea. I think I know how it should be now. Tomorrow is my day off. I guess Vance Lee and I will go on a little trip, maybe over to the east coast. Fifteen victories for the group today.

April 22nd ...

Today Lee and I hitchhiked from San Severo to a town on the Adriatic Sea. There were two large lakes near the coast with sail boats cruising around. The Adriatic looks about like the Mediterranean, maybe not as blue. We took some pictures. We decided to come back from there by train so we caught it at a little junction. We rode up in the cab with the engineer and fireman. Quite an experience. On the way back, the wheels got spinning on a little incline and we had to get out and put sand on the rails. We averaged about 15 miles an hour on the way back.

We got back at camp just at dark. We hadn't eaten all day so we cooked six eggs we had purchased from the engineer, toasted some bread and ate some cheese. We got sort of dirty in the engine but we enjoyed the trip a lot.

April 23rd ...

Worked on the walls of the shower today while our pilots went to Weiner Neudstadt in Austria.

April 24th ...

Today Bain and I got two of our drums welded together that we plan to use for heating the water. Tomorrow we may finish it. No mission today.

April 26th ...

It rained all day today so we didn't do anything but read and sleep. We did put up part of the shower room walls during a break however. And if it's nice tomorrow, we can finish it all.

April 27th ...

It rained again today but Bain and I managed to get some more work done on our shower. Maybe we'll get it finished one of these days, I hope.

April 30th ...

Today was payday and I drew the $10.20 as usual. I changed my allotment so I'll be drawing a little more ... some more to lose in card games. Bain and I are still working on our shower. We don't plan to charge admission anymore but plan to build an annex onto it and sleep there. Room with adjoining bath, you know. Snazzy. Our pilots are flying missions regularly over Germany and occupied territory. Getting some and losing some. Today the group was assembled for a medal-presenting ordeal. Some General presented them.

May 3rd 1944 ...

We have just about finished our shower and it's really nice. Electric lights, running water in a wash basin (helmet,) toilet article cabinet, etc.

May 6ᵗʰ ...

I decided to make a clothes cabinet today for the shower room ... then my clothes won't get so dusty. Now that we have a stove in the shower, Bob Savage and I take a shower each morning after we run the mile and a half. I always take one at night, too. I hope my soap holds out.

May 9ᵗʰ ...

I got some corrected papers back from Penn State, and the marks showed good to better. Our pilots are still flying 4, 5 and 6 hour missions. It must be rough.

May 11ᵗʰ ...

Tonight we heard we are restricted to the Post and that everywhere is off limits. Can't understand it unless the invasion is due soon. We (Lee, Savage and I) had planned a fishing trip for tomorrow, our day off. Finito, I guess.

May 12ᵗʰ ...

This morning it seemed the "off limits" was just a scare. Lee, Savage and I left at 9:00 a.m. with duffle bag and bed roll for a lake near the Adriatic Sea. In three rides we were at the lake and bartering with some kids for a boat. We couldn't talk them into letting us take the boat ourselves, so we went across the lake with some old fishermen who were going over to fish. They told us our best chances of catching any fish would be in the Adriatic. So ... we toted our equipment over land about a mile. It was about 2:00 p.m. when we arrived here so we ate some salmon, toast, butter and coffee.

We cast our "River Runt Spook" plug from the shore, attempted to manage a boat in the rough surf, failed. About 7:00 p.m. we started to cook our supper. We had purchased some onions from an old lady so I put them in the bottom of my mess kit and let them simmer in butter. Then we put in some Vienna sausages and cooked them 'til brown. These, on a piece of buttered toast, tasted like something cooked for the Gods. We munched these to near capacity, drank some coffee and finished off with peaches and cream, and a cigarette. A log-fire cooked meal always tastes better, especially if there is some sand and bugs in it. We laid around the fire until 10:30 p.m. and talked, the first we'd done this since the U.S.

May 13ᵗʰ ...
We got up this morning at 5:00 a.m. in preparation for going fishing with some Italian fishermen who use nets. We cooked three eggs each and had toast and coffee with them. Very, very good. The surf was rough so we didn't go out in the boat. We did cast more from the shore, however, but all efforts were in vain. We enjoyed being out even if we didn't catch anything. About 10:00 a.m., we started back for the little fishing village from where we first left in the boat. We got there at 11:30 a.m. and, after catching two rides, we were back in camp at 2:00 p.m. The fishermen gave us some fish we will check on tonight. The trip I enjoyed a lot. I hope the pictures I took of it come out O.K..

May 16ᵗʰ ...
Bob Savage and I are still running mornings before we have breakfast. We run a mile and a half, take a shower and go to chow. It really makes me feel good. It seems like I want to be doing something all day. Very invigorating. I go into San Severo to the Gym quite a few nights a week and limber up, too ... lift weights, skip rope, etc.

May 20ᵗʰ ...
Today I was off and a bunch of us went jeeping about the

country. Went to Manfradonia, Foggia, San Severo, Apricena, over to the Adriatic and elsewhere. Quite a ride ... my nose got sunburned.

May 28th ...

We were released this p.m. so Marsh and I went to Foggia to a track meet. I enjoyed it very much. The fastest mile was 5:21, not very fast. We went to a good jam session afterwards.

May 29th ...

Just for curiosity's sake, I timed myself for the mile this morning and it was 5:47 ... not good but I'm not in shape. The road where we run is very rough, too.

May 30th ...

I went to San Severo to the Gym again tonight. Tomorrow is payday. I have 9 lire left ......

June 1st 1944 ...

Today three guys from our Squadron left on detached service (d.s.). for some place. It seems to be quite a secret. Today Marsh and I bummed to Termoli on the Adriatic Sea and went swimming ... my first swim in that sea.

June 3rd ...

It was announced today on the radio that bombers and fighters of the 15th Air Force (that's us) landed in Russia, refueled and came back. We guess that's where the three guys went. Would I ever like to go there on a deal like that ......

June 4th ...

Two years ago today we were crossing the Atlantic to England. What a stretch we are putting in over here!!! Ran the mile in 6:6 tonight.

June 6ᵗʰ ...
D-Day
The Allies landed at Normandie, Southern France coast today. Fierce fighting.

June 7ᵗʰ ...
The Italian people are harvesting their grain now. The fields stretch for miles and miles, and I enjoy the walks I take about every night. I always did like to be outside with nature, I guess.

June 10ᵗʰ ...
I ran down the road a piece tonight, ran the half-mile in 2:30. O.K. for the place I did it. I wish I was where I could practice. I'd like to know if I could ever run the mile very fast. Someday maybe I can train and find out.

June 12ᵗʰ ...
Maybe tomorrow Bain and I will go down south to Taranto to a bomber field where he knows a fellow. Should be a nice trip.

June 13ᵗʰ ...
Today, as planned, Bill and I hitchhiked south through Bari and Taranto to Manduria, the place where the bomber field is located. We stopped in Bari at the *Red Cross Club* for coffee and cakes and started out again. We caught rides in about every kind of vehicle the Allies have. Took some pictures in Taranto but didn't spend much time there. We saw very few Americans, mostly Italian sailors. It's a very large port, the place of the naval engagement between the English and the Eyties some years ago.

From there we went to the field only to find Bill's friend was forced down. However, we had supper there and found a place to sleep all night. About 9:00 p.m. we went to the Officers' Quarters and talked to some of the pilots who knew Bill's friend, Baker. Some of them had over 40 missions and they were really gone. That's a tough job for the nerves ... flak, fighters, storms, etc. take their toll. At 11:00 p.m. we went to some of the crews' barracks and slept in vacant beds.

June 14th ...

Got up at 6:00 a.m. this morning, had chow and went out to the line to watch the big ones take off on a mission. At about 10:30 a.m. we were sweating out the courier for a ride north when a stripped *B-17E* came in that was eventually landing at San Severo, a break. Bill and I got up in the plexiglass nose and laid and sat there all the way back. What a view we could get from there. I plugged in a head set and listened to some Foggia swing music until we got too far away, then I tuned in Naples. On the way there we buzzed low over the Vesuvius crater. The top of it looks much different than it did when we climbed up it last fall. There was just a little sulphur-looking smoke rising from its depths. We landed on a field outside of Caserta, had dinner there and flew from there to four miles from San Severo at about 4:30 p.m. We bummed from there back to camp and got there in time for a shower and then supper. I took some pictures along the way. All in all, it was a swell trip.

June 19th ...

Ran down the road a piece again tonight. I"ve been doing this quite a bit lately. I'd like to be near a track where I could practice a lot. I think I'd like to do some track work some day.

June 23ʳᵈ ...
Some of the boys from the Squadron are going to Rome ... not legally, but going. I certainly don't want to miss going there. Maybe I should go one of these days.

June 25ᵗʰ ...
I ran a half mile in 2:28 tonight. The road is very rough, making it harder to run on than a cinder track. I'd like to train with a little coaching for two or three months on a good track and see if there is any speed in me. I'm almost positive I can build up enough endurance. I don't smoke or drink coffee anymore, if that helps. I never did get much excitement from smoking ... might just as well quit, I guess.

June 26ᵗʰ ...
Leroy Marsh of California and I plan to get a 24-hour pass tomorrow and go to Rome. We can get a plane ride most of the way, we think. I got some K-Rations from the Quartermaster out back of our area to take along just in case we have a hard time getting anything to eat. We've heard finding a place to stay and food is quite a problem. We'll see. We leave in the morning at 6:30 a.m.

June 27ᵗʰ ...
Leroy and I got up this morning at 5:30 a.m. and had Harned take us down to the field so we could catch the *B-25* courier at 6:30 a.m. for a drome near Rome. We were very lucky to get on it and left at 6:45, Leroy up front and me in the rear, holding oxygen bottles from slipping around. After a while in the air I sat on a stool between two windows and watched things below pass by. Saw some bomb craters by the roads in the mountains where they fought so hard last winter.

After flying a little over an hour at 220 mph, we landed at

a field on the beach about 65 miles northwest of Rome. We got out on the road and after several rides, got to Rome about 12:30 p.m. The road north of Rome is very beautiful, tree lined, and winding and hilly. Looked a little like some roads in the States.

The first thing we did on arriving was to find a place to stay over night. That was our main concern at first. We found a private home that we could stay at for a dollar each. We were a stones throw from the *Pantheon*, supposedly Rome's most perfect building. Later on we walked around town viewing and taking pictures. We saw Victor Emanuel's monument, Mussolini's balcony and square, the Colosseum, Roman Forum, Caesar's Forum, Arch of Constantine, the Tiber, Tomb of St. Angelo, St. Peter's (from a distance), etc.

We left our field bags (with K-Rations, toilet articles, etc.) at the *Red Cross Club*. It really is a nice building, an elaborate pre-war hotel. We stayed at the *Red Cross Club* until 9:00 p.m. and then went to the house. It was a nice room we had, and enjoyed the night's sleep after walking so much.

June 28th ...

This morning we got up at 8:00 a.m., went to the *Red Cross Club*, ate our K-Rations, and started around town again. We went first to St. Peter Cathedral, the largest in the world, and went through it from bottom to top. We went clear into the round ball on the very peak of the dome, went up a ladder to see out the slit openings in it, and look over the city. We took some pictures in and around it and very, very much impressed by the greatness of it all.

After seeing this, we figured the rest of the time (we had to start back by noon) we'd shop around for souvenirs, etc. After buying some light bulbs, etc., we packed our field bags and started for Littoria Airfield where we would try to get a

80

ride back to, at least, Naples. The second *C-47* pilot we asked would take us and we took off at 2:30 p.m. On taking off, he circled completely around Rome and we got a perfect bird's eye view. On the way back he also flew over Cassino and the famous Abbey, and what a bunch of rubble that looked to be. We got to a field near Naples at 3:45 p.m. and tried the rest of the day to get a ride to Foggia, but to no avail, and it was too late to hitchhike across. What a predicament ... we were due at camp the next morning. We figured our only alternative would be to stay all night at the hospital nearby at Aversa and try to catch the Courier back to San Severo in the morning.

June 29th ...
So, at 4:30 a.m., we got up and went to the airfield. As it happened, the Courier left from one side of the field when we were at the other. What luck ... I felt much dejected. After this happened, there was but one thing to do ... bum back. So-o-o-o ... we started back the long way. We caught Eytie-driven G.I. trucks, English convoys, amphibious Jeeps, Jeeps, etc., and finally caught a Command car for the majority of the way. We arrived at Foggia at 1:00 p.m. and at the line at 2:30 p.m., expecting to be much reprimanded for over-staying our pass by 26 hours. As it turned out, our Communications Officer and Section head were both gone and the First Sergeant chose not to punish us. What a break ... and what a trip! I'll never forget it.

June 30th ...
Today was payday ... just got back in time. I can use the $25.20 I get.

July 3rd 1944 ...
Our planes and pilots are still going on those long missions to Ploesti, Bucharest, Austria, Toulon, and

elsewhere. With all the land front news these missions just get back page mention now. We are certainly in a rut, up at 5:30 a.m. every morning, back for chow at 11:00, back to the line 'til 3:00 p.m., and back to the area for a shower and rest before supper at about 5:30 p.m. There is a show on every other night here on the post, a few ball games, but other than this our recreation is much limited. Well, we'll enjoy going home more, I guess. A few of the fellows are going home now on rotation. The war will be over before I get the chance though, I bet.

July 7ᵗʰ ...
I still run down the road a piece at night. Keeping limbered up.

August 30ᵗʰ 1944 ...
Bill Bain and I are talking of building our house here now that it's rumored we may be here for some time longer.

September 4ᵗʰ 1944 ...
I just got back from a 3-day leave at the rest camp in Manfradonia. Woody Pemberton and I were the two radio men to go. We swam, bought melons, went to town and played tennis. It was the first tennis I've played since I've been overseas. Pretty rusty. I got some track time in on the beach. The food was good and, all in all, I enjoyed the stay very much.

September 10ᵗʰ ...
Bill and I have been collecting more boards in preparation for our house.

September 12ᵗʰ ...
We started today on our house, nailed a few sides together. Prefabricated job, it is.

September 13th ...
We put up our prefabricated sides today and our house looks like it will be quite large.

September 14th ...
Put part of the floor down today and some of the roof. We are both off tomorrow and plan to do much on it.

September 15th ...
Last night after dark I was climbing on our shower platform and fell off backwards. I sprained my ankle pretty bad and limped around today, so didn't work like a beaver as I planned. However, we got some double siding done and can move in tomorrow. I'm making a chair with our radio mounted on one arm. It will be about done tomorrow and our house will be up so I can move it into the house instead of into the tent where we've been living.

September 16th ...
My ankle is still stiff but coming along fine. We moved in tonight and I think we have a nice house. We haven't waterproofed our roof yet. I hope it doesn't rain.

September 17th ...
This p.m. it rained and we were busy keeping things dry in our leaking house. At night we went to Foggia and went to a stage show starring Katherine Cornell and Brian Ahern. Very good it was.

September 18th ...
Today Bill and I waterproofed our roof ... we used dope and fabric strips. I made a door frame and put our door up. Went to a show at night. We may install a fireplace. What luxuries we have in this house!

September 19ᵗʰ ...

Worked on our house 'til dark and then went to a show. A hot shower and to bed at 10:30 p.m.

September 20ᵗʰ ...

Last night at the show they told us there would be an English blood collecting unit her tomorrow and everybody with Type O should donate a pint. So today at 1:15 p.m. I was lying on a cot with a needle in my arm. It took about ten minutes and I'm glad I have been a blood donor. According to the medic who extracted the blood from me, the blood taken from us today will be in some wounded soldier by tomorrow night. They say raw blood is better than plasma in that it is quicker acting. They store it in refrigerators until used.

I got a bottle of English beer as a reward but couldn't drink it. I don't see how we developed a taste for that while in England. We could get $10 for the pint we donated but I'm not going to ask for it. I'm grateful if I can help save a dying infantryman at the front.

I worked on my bunk in the afternoon and nearly finished it. I got some springs to make a bed with.

September 24ᵗʰ ...

We oiled our floor today and it looks good. I think I'll oil my bunk when I finish it. It's about finished now. I have the clock mounted in one end (by my head) and four switches controlling radio, lights, etc., on the side to balance it. I have a light in the corner that can be either in direct or indirect lighting. We plan to get some paint and paint the inside walls. I developed some pictures (film) tonight. I've received much stuff from home to do this work with. I don't work at it as much as I did.

September 26th ...
I have my spring bed completed now and it looks buono.
We painted the door and finished stripping the cracks outside.

September 27th ...
We have all of our house double-sided now, the windows
and all. It should be real warm this winter. Our chair is quite
the thing. Much comment on it, mostly good. It is something
definitely different than anything we've been seeing for some
time.
The Squadron is fixing up our mess hall and day room.
Already the mess hall looks better. In the bar we are to get a
circular bar and many other fancy things, maybe snacks two
or three times a week.

September 29th ...
Today we were told there is to be an inspection
(personnel) some day next week by the Commanding General
of this Wing. Maybe drill, too, for a while. What a war ....
We painted the inside of our house today (a beige) and I
oil-painted my bunk. Tomorrow is pay day. It rained again
today ... much rain lately.

October 2nd 1944 ...
Wow, what a day. It was raining when we got up this
morning and it didn't stop all day. It rained hard, too. We are
in for some inclement weather for a while now, I guess. As
nice as our house is, I still get uneasy in it. Too much sack
time, accomplished little ....

October 3rd ...
Rained today, not as steady. I'm on guard tomorrow
morning from 4:00 to 8:00 a.m. To bed at 9:30 p.m.

October 4th ...

When the Sergeant of the Guard woke me it wasn't raining. I put all my wool flying clothes on over my O.D.'s and didn't get very cold. I made plans how to build the fireplace I'm going to attempt and when the sun came up at 6:00 a.m., the sky was clear of clouds. So we had our first mission in days. They went to Munich, saw nothing. The World Series started today and at 7:45 p.m., (12:45 CST) we were naturally tuned in. We do like to hear the games being announced ... it's so few we hear. The *St. Louis Browns* won the opener two to one.

October 5th ...

Well, I slept the latest this morning that I have since I've been over here, I think ... until 9:15 a.m. It was my day off and raining. Bill got up early and left for Rome and I slept on. It's the first time I've missed breakfast since Oran, I think. I got up and started our gas can fire and read, etc. all day. Rain ... rain ... rain ... what weather. Bill and I just got our house up in time for a number of reasons ... our new Executive Officer says no more houses and with all this rainy weather our planes aren't flying, therefore no wing tank boxes to work with, and also all the rainy weather we never could have been working ... just in time! Sometimes I think I'm lucky in many respects. I hope it continues.

October 8th ...

Many inspections lately. One of the quarters coming up soon, I guess. Our C.O. had the Group C.O. over inspecting our shack this morning.

October 11th ...

Today our pilots went on a strafing mission in southern

Germany. We lost our C.O. and many others of the planes got shot up. One got hit by an 88 which nearly blew the wing off. He ran into a tree but came back with fir needles in the wings. One of the transportation boys started the fire in the shower today and nearly burned down the platform. I'll have to fix it on my day off tomorrow.

October 12th ...

Today Bill and I repaired the shower platform and put a layer of brick underneath the fire-pot of the hot water barrels. I worked in my dark room some at night. Today the Group got cited by the President, the second time. Lt. General Twining made the award. I watched from our house ... we were supposed to be in the assembly.

October 14th ...

Bill and I are really going to build a fireplace. We've been undecided until now. We have the brick and some sand, and will start soon.

October 15th ...

Today I cut a hole in the floor the size the fireplace will be.

October 16th ...

Bill and I were off today so we put in the foundation and part of the upright of our fireplace. I've never done any masonry work before so I guess the job will be a long one.

October 18th ...

We worked tonight on the fireplace, got some more done. I'm checking on a cabin building book I have for pointers occasionally. Much comment on it by different fellows. I hope it works O.K..

October 21ˢᵗ ...

Still working on our fireplace ... slowly but surely we'll finish it.

October 23ʳᵈ ...

My ankle is still swelled from when I sprained it weeks ago. I haven't been able to run any lately due to this. However, I've been out occasionally trying to limber up.

October 26ᵗʰ ...

Today Bill and I were both off so, in the forenoon, we worked on the fireplace and, in the p.m., went to Foggia to a show and the *Red Cross Club*. It was the first time I've been off the Post for a couple months. No place to go. I'm about due for a Rome trip soon. We got back in time for chow (6:00 p.m.) and me to go on guard at 7:00 p.m. While on guard I watched a show in our new theater. I was supposed to be on guard until 1:30 a.m. but decided there was no reason for a guard on a bucket of charcoal, and went to bed. I also sent a much-delayed package home today.

October 27ᵗʰ ...

I was off this a.m. on account of guard last night and I put up some chimney. Should finish it soon.

October 28ᵗʰ ...

Today, this p.m., Bill and I ran the chimney up through the roof and at night had a homey little wood fire in our completed fireplace. A job well done. It seems to work O.K..

November 1ˢᵗ 1944 ...

Got paid yesterday and today I got my first Christmas package. One from Lela and one from Ethel Speros.

November 4th ...

Now that our fireplace is completed and in operation, burning wood, we chop up some each night, just like back home. It's good exercise, too. On my last day off I finished the fire-place inside and out. Although there is much heat loss, it still heats our house good.

November 5th ...

Just to show what can and does happen to us occasionally ... today when I was at the dinner table I was told I could fly to Rome for a five day rest period if the fellow who was scheduled to go didn't get back to camp by 1:00 p.m. I was a little skeptical but thought I would accept. So at 12:15 p.m., I was changing clothes, readying myself for a plane trip to Rome. Just as I got all my things packed and dressed, this fellow returned. What a life ... well, I'll be going in a few days.

November 12th ...

The Rome trip is coming up tomorrow and I think I'll go to Florence instead. I went to Base Operations today and inquired as to a plane to there. The Courier goes from here to Florence with no stops. It leaves at 10:30 a.m. and gets there about 12:15 p.m. which is very good if we caught a ride on it. Leroy Marsh and Moe Harris will go with me. They have three-day passes. I worked some more on my electric door opener tonight and it works O.K..

November 13th ...

This morning at 9:00 a.m. we went to the field and were lucky enough to get on the Courier (*C-47*) for Florence. We left at 10:30 a.m. and arrived at Firenze (Florence) about 12:15 p.m., a very cold ride it was. We flew over the mountains in Eastern and Central Italy, snow covered. The airdrome we landed at was three miles from town so we were in Florence in a short time.

We inquired as to a *Red Cross Club* and found one down in the center of town. It was well-populated with 5th Army Infantry men. We checked some of our field bags and set forth to find a place to stay. We went from one apartment to another until at last we found a family who had a double and a single, so we took it. We told them we'd be back at 9:00 p.m., paid the dollar, and took off for the *Red Cross Club* again. We didn't eat any dinner and for supper had coffee and cakes. It seems there is only one G.I. restaurant in town and a pass is necessary to eat there. We don't have passes so eating may become a problem before we leave here.

We spent the evening around the Club listening to an Eytie band, etc., and at 8:30 p.m. started out in a totally dark city for the walk across town to our room. Leroy had a flashlight and without much trouble, we got back O.K.. This family seems like a nice bunch of people. One of the girls is studying English. We (Leroy is our chief interpreter) visited with them a while and then went to bed. I took the single and it was a pretty good bed. We plan on a tour tomorrow.

November 14th ...

We got up at 8:30 a.m. this morning, washed and walked to the *Red Cross Club* for coffee and cakes again. After this we bought some things in different stores. I got an ash tray, copper dinner bell, some mosaic brooches and bracelets. At noon, Leroy went to the 5th Army restaurant and ate while Moe and I went back for coffee and cookies. We've also been eating some peanuts we'd brought along.

In the p.m. we went on a tour of Florence with a Red Cross woman. She took us to the outskirts of the town first to a monastery which proved to be quite interesting. It commanded a good view of Florence and the River Arno. Near here we saw an old amphitheater, one used by the Etruscans, an ancient warring tribe. From there we went back towards town and then to another side of town to a large cathedral, the San Miniato. The outskirts of Florence (suburbs) are beautiful. There are many hills around Florence, and the rich have villas here. Many Americans own some here. From this cathedral we drove around some and to a few more places of interest.

To the *Red Cross Club* at 5:30 p.m. We went to the airdrome to an engineering outfit and had supper, the first warm meal in two days. From there we went back downtown and walked for a half hour in the rain trying to find a theater which had a stage show. We finally found it and saw the last half of it. At 8:30 we went back to the room.

These seem like nice people. The people up north here seem more civilized and more modern than those farther south. Florence is beat up quite a bit, especially along the Arno River. All the original bridges have been blown up but one. This is the famous Ponte Vecchio, the one with stores, etc. on it. We plan on visiting it before we leave. There are two or three Bailey bridges across the Arno however. Tomorrow we plan on hitch-hiking to Pisa to see the famous Tower. It is about fifty miles, I guess.

November 15th ...
This morning at 8:00 a.m. we got up and started for Pisa. We caught a number of rides and enjoyed the trip very much. The road runs along the Arno for quite some distance. At about noon we got to Pisa and a beat-up town we found it to be. On the opposite side of the river from the Tower was the worst. Every building was hit, I think. We stopped at a Fighter Group and had dinner, then went to the Tower.

We were much impressed when we first saw the Tower. It leans 16' out of perpendicular. We walked up the spiraling stairway to the top and found the wind blowing like heck. We had to hang on or get blown off. I didn't make many observations as did Galileo. While here, we visited a large cathedral on the same grounds as the Tower. This was a beautiful place and it contained some fine mosaics, paintings and sculpturing. Also here (and we saw it) was hanging the same lamp that Galileo looked at and got the idea for the pendulum. After taking some pictures here and buying some souvenirs we took off for Florence. Regardless of blown-up bridges, high water (Arno), etc., we got there about dark.

We ate at a quartermaster outfit at the outskirts of Florence. From there we went to the theater where the stage show was, trying to see what the first half of that show was. Well, we got there at about the same time as the night previous. What luck. Went back to the room and looked at books, pictures, etc. and drank their vino 'til 9:30 p.m. when we went to bed. Tomorrow p.m. we plan to start for Foggia.

November 16th ...

This morning we went downtown and shopped quite a bit. I bought some more mosaic brooches and bracelets, a couple letter openers, some post cards and an alabaster and marble night light which I will send home sometime. At about noon we started for the field to catch a plane for somewhere south. At 1:30 p.m. we caught a hospital ship which was going to Naples, 350 miles away. About 15 minutes after we had landed in Naples we were in a *B-24* headed for 20 miles south of Foggia. We arrived there at dusk, ate supper and caught a truck for Foggia about an hour later. After a few truck rides, we got back to camp at 8:30 p.m. All in all, this was a very successful trip and I have a bunch of nice souvenirs to send home and elsewhere.

November 17th ...
My Rome pass is still in effect today so I took it and worked around the house here straightening up, etc.

November 19th ...
I have the Florence and Pisa souvenirs up on the ledge around my bunk and on the fireplace mantel. The night light, which is made of alabaster and is of two polar bears on a piece of ice, is quite the thing. It looks good on the fireplace mantel.

November 23rd ...
We played volley ball today at noon. We usually do this after chow each noon. It's a form of exercise so I go out and jump around a bit.

November 26th ...
Bill thinks he may be able to go home on account of his father's illness. He has the orderly room and group working on it. For his own good, I hope he can make it. Although I'll hate to see him go.

November 30th ...
Today was payday and I am a few bucks richer. Leroy Marsh paid me $20 he owed me, also Powell $10. It seems I have plenty of money now that I had my allotment lowered sometime back.

December 3rd 1944 ...
Today I am 25 years old. Gosh, it seems I'm getting old ... not physically though, and that's the main thing, I guess. I haven't been running so much lately as my ankle still hurts some and it's been raining quite a bit.

December 6th ...

Mom sent a couple wreaths in a package and I have them up here in our house, one on the fireplace and the other in a corner. Also, I got some pine boughs with tinsel up here on the walls, etc.

December 10th ...

I planned to go over and see Pappy Hale today, this being my day off, but it rained so I didn't. I'll make it yet.

December 12th ...

Bill has it made, I guess. He is to go on rotation about the 17th of this month. He surely is lucky. I guess C.V. Taylor will move in, in his place.

December 14th ...

Our house is well decorated for Christmas ... wreaths, pine boughs, tinsel, etc. I took some inside shots of it and they came out fairly good.

December 16th ...

Bill leaves tomorrow. Goes to Bari, then Naples. He came down with Malaria yesterday and was real sick, but I guess he will make it.

December 17th ...

Bill got up this morning feeling pretty good and raring to go. He left at 8:00 a.m. I hated to see him go, sorta'.

December 20th ...

I went over to see Pappy Hale today on my day off. I had dinner there and rode back with a Red Cross doughnut girl at 4:00 p.m. Got back for supper ... pork chops, too.

December 25th ...

Today ... yep ... today is Christmas. I'm going by the calendar ... I wouldn't know otherwise. Had a mission today and our big meal at supper, everything from turkey to dates. May be home by next Christmas. Hope so!

Chapter Four
1945

January 1ˢᵗ 1945 ...

Much gun firing last night. Another big meal today.

January 5ᵗʰ ...

Today Pappy Hale came over and will stay all night with me. He thought our house was pretty much O.K..

January 6ᵗʰ ...

This afternoon Pappy went back. He was on a 5-day pass and was due back tomorrow. We have been inquiring lately as to going deer hunting up in some woods beyond San Marco and San Angelo. Some fellows in the other squadrons have been, and got a couple. They are real small, like gazelles. We rushed around this afternoon and night getting our three-day passes, chow, transportation, guns, ammo, candles, etc. If things work out O.K., we will leave in the morning.

January 7ᵗʰ ...

This morning at 5:00 a.m., I arose and woke up the other four fellows, Warren Lints, Red Schnelling, Doc Savage and Keith Hill. We ate breakfast and then packed our tent, food, bedding, cooking utensils, guns, etc. on a trailer and by 8:00 a.m. were ready to go. We went through Foggia and got our hunting passes. After a long pull up the mountains, we ran into some snow (down and coming down). We went about 50

96

miles and finally got to some decent-sized trees, the first large ones I'd seen in Italia. Most were beech and three and four foot through. We drove up a trail 200 yards and put up our tent. After this, at about 3:00 p.m., we sighted our rifles and took off to see in what direction we should go tomorrow. Nearby it looked pretty well populated by goats, pigs, etc. It really seemed out of this world, hunting in big timber again. I borrowed a Mauser so was well prepared.

About dark we all wandered back and started to cook supper. We all made something and had fried potatoes (in bacon strips), peas and corn, toast and butter, and good coffee with cream, sugar and ashes. Sat around reminiscing 'til 9:00 p.m.

January 8ᵗʰ ...

My alarm clock started raising hell at 5:00 a.m. this morning so I hopped up, started the fire and hollered at the rest of the guys. Warren got up and we started to cook breakfast. The gas can went dry and, in transferring gasoline while in the tent, it caught fire and during the next five minutes everyone was busy. I had a 5-gallon can of gas in my hand when it caught and I went backwards out of the door with it. My boots caught fire but I soon put them out. There was gasoline burning in the doorway and Doc Savage grabbed the two comforters and a blanket from my sack and tried to smother it out before it burned down the tent. He did a good job ... not on the comforters ... and we got it out with it burning only one tent flap. This was a very dumb thing for Warren and me to do; however, we got it out before it did much damage and it may be a lesson to us.

We eventually had bacon and eggs, toast and coffee before starting out at dawn. Hill stayed behind to watch the tent ... tomorrow, it's me. Red and I started down one ridge and Warren and Doc went down another. As we weren't in the

97

tall timber, I started to bear to the right after going about a mile and worked up a valley. Finally got to the top and decided to sit a while, rest and wait. I sat on a log for about fifteen minutes, ate a candy bar and left, when ... to my disgust ... an Eytie came up through the woods driving a herd of pigs. What a place.

I walked up an old log trail for about another mile and came out on the main road. I decided to walk the road until I caught a ride down to the tall timber. Got a ride with some other G.I. hunters to an English-occupied Italian lodge. This kind of country looked more like what is back home ... big trees, much holly and snow here in the big stuff.

I walked down another log trail a way, then off it a couple hundred yards, and sat on another log for an hour and a half. Sitting there in the woods, smelling the damp leaves and what-ever else that makes up a woods smell, and watching the chickadees and snow birds hopping around, topped by the tap of a woodpecker occasionally, is certainly in my medium. I loved it.

As for deer, I saw none and moved farther back into the timber and sat on an upturned tree stump. There was very little shooting and few hunters, so if there were many deer in the woods they weren't moving much.

I left there in a short time and started for camp which was about five miles away. I saw many deer tracks, but nothing that could make them. Saw some rabbit and squirrel tracks, too. I was very tired when I finally arrived at camp about 3:00 p.m.

The rest of the fellows had gotten back and with the same luck I'd had. They were making coffee and toasting bread, so I fell in line and boosted my spirits with some java. As I will say again and again, you can't beat coffee made over a wood fire out in the woods. Much of it is psychological, I suppose.

Soon afterwards we started supper and, by dark, we were eating fried potatoes and bacon, peas and corn, bread, apple butter, toast, coffee, etc. Good beyond explanation was that meal.

After we had finished we sat around and reminisced on other hunting and fishing expeditions until the candles burned out. I put my leather flying clothes on at night as I had few blankets because of the fire to cover up with. By morning, I was shivering very much and didn't rest too much all night.

January 9th ...

The other fellows got up at 6:30 a.m. this morning, but not me as it was my day to stay in camp. They cooked bacon and eggs, toasted bread, and made coffee. After they left I got up and had the same. I spent the forenoon straightening things up. Took a count of the food we had left and gathered more chips for the fire we kept going all day.

About 11:00 a.m., Doc Savage came back sick at his stomach. As long as he would be in the tent, I figured I might as well go out hunting again. I crossed a valley near our camp site and sat nearly to the top of a ridge until another Eytie came driving some pigs through the woods. This made me very disgusted and I shouldered my rifle and walked back to camp.

When I arrived, I found all the fellows there, including Redwine. He had the truck and said we could go back tonight if we wanted to. We cooked some coffee and toasted some bread and took some pictures of it all. We decided to go back before dark and also decided we wouldn't need the ammunition we had left, so we started the damndest racket one ever heard. We were shooting Mauser's, Springfield's, Carbine's and a .45. Birds, trees, leaves and C-Ration cans got hell for about half an hour.

After all our shells were gone we started to pack our bed rolls, chow, utensils, tent, etc. I got mine packed first so I took the remaining can of milk and some tomato puree, and made some "most delicious" tomato soup. We all had a cup of this and a cup of coffee, and started back. We put the trailer in the back of the truck and got in ourselves. On the way back, Doc Savage got sick again and vomited, and then felt better. We got back to camp about 9:00 p.m., wet, dirty, and without any game. Warren and I took a shower and went to bed.

January 10th ...

I had to go to the line today and didn't get to sew up the tent. I borrowed it from one of the other Squadrons and feel that I should fix it up before returning it. None of the other fellows are very eager to help, so it looks like it's my job, and what a job it will be.

January 11th ...

All day today I sewed on that damn tent and finished it about 3:00 p.m., then took it back. As I figured, I did it alone.

January 15th ...

I heard from Ralph Apple today. He is sweating out being transferred to the infantry. That's one of the disadvantages of going home on rotation ... they need infantrymen now. I might take a furlough when the weather gets better back home, maybe May. Could help Dad then.

January 17th ...

The ducks and geese fly over our camp here by the hundreds. Wish I could get a shotgun and shells. I'd like to go hunting them. Some of the fellows are going out but not having exceptional luck.

January 21ˢᵗ ...

Today I made a box for the "bears" centerpiece. Now to get it censored and sent. I don't have much stuff here to send now.

January 22ⁿᵈ ...

I was off today and I tore my darkroom down. It looked sort of dilapidated and the little work I do I can do in the shower at night. I had to do some rewiring, too.

January 25ᵗʰ ...

I finished the desk lamp I have been working on for sometime. Because the power is erratic, I decided to fix a lamp with both an electric and a battery bulb in it. I have a storage battery here for the door opener anyway.

January 26ᵗʰ ...

I went and had my teeth checked today and found I had two cavities so had same fixed. That's service ... and no cost either.

January 28ᵗʰ ...

Today C.V. and I went and got a load of gravel and put it in a mud hole in our front yard. The land here in camp is so flat that the water nearly lays where it falls. Very poor drainage system. Now that it rains quite a bit the water isn't soaking in and all the low spots are full all the time.

January 29ᵗʰ ...

Last night it started snowing and is still coming down today. There is about 4" on the ground now. We had some snowball fights today. I took some pictures.

February 2nd 1945 ...

It was real nice today, like spring. Since the *Blue Room* serves ice cream, we go in to San Severo quite often in the afternoon after the planes come back, and eat and eat. They have delicious fried eggs, french fried potatoes, a salad, a parker house roll and coffee lunches also. We usually eat two or three orders of these and that many dishes of ice cream, and come back to camp and forget about supper here. Our suppers on the post aren't too bad, but the lunches are quite light.

February 4th ...

Went to the *Blue Room* again this afternoon for ice cream, etc. Came back to camp to a show at 5:30 p.m.

February 5th ...

They are going to have Psychology classes here on the post and I plan to attend them. It is either go to a class or drill. Anyway, I want to study this if I can. It may supplement my extension course. I haven't been studying my Psychology course from Penn State like I should. I'm on lesson 9 now.

February 7th ...

C.V. left for Rome today on a 7-day pass. I broke a corner of one of my teeth and went and had it filled today. It was a terribly big hole before the Doc put the filling in it.

February 8th ...

Tonight I got a fellow with a good camera to take some time exposure shots in the house. I fixed up three 100-watt bulbs for lighting.

February 10th ...

Tonight when I got back from more ice cream and tuna

fish dinners at the *Blue Room* I developed three rolls of film I have had. Most of them came out good ... the shots inside the house, the snowball fights and those taken up in the "deer woods." A *B-24* bomber was forced down on our field tonight and the crew is sleeping in different tents in our Squadron. One of them, the ball turret gunner, is staying with me, sleeping in C.V.'s bed.

February 11th ...

The gunner is staying with me again tonight, I guess. I sent the polar bear centerpiece home today, also the two fish from Pisa and an ash tray from Florence.

February 12th ...

This afternoon three of us went into town to the *Blue Room* on the way back from the line. The ice cream was the best yet. Had three orders of bacon and eggs, etc. too. When I got back to camp by way of a gravel truck at 6:00 p.m., I went to a Psychology class. Guess I'll go to these now, may learn something there. Got four letters but the lights went off at 9:00 p.m. and my battery is getting down so I guess I won't answer any tonight. While in town today, I got three lace dress collars I'll send home soon. Such prices these things have on them.

February 13th ...

Went to the *Blue Room* again at 4:00 p.m. Got back for weekly orientation in the Club room at 6:00 p.m. Guarded a gas can fire from 10:00 p.m. to 2:00 a.m. at the front gate. Tomorrow I'm off. Think I'll go to the line anyway and finish my steam cabinet. It's about done.

February 15th ...

Had a bad crack-up on the field today. A *P-51* mushed-in on the takeoff and crashed through a South African maintenance shop, a tent and two trucks. It killed at least five and injured that many more. A terrible thing. I helped check the runway lights tonight before we came back to the area at 4:30 p.m. Went after gasoline today to San Severo and got ice cream while there.

February 17th ...
One fellow (radio) left on a 30-day furlough today. If things continue as they are, I may return in May. Went to the *Blue Room* again this afternoon for ice cream. At night I took the first bath in my newly constructed steam cabinet. It worked O.K.. I sweated much, got some cleaner, I guess. There are some horrible rumors around about moving a couple hundred miles up the coast. What a sad thing that will be ... leaving this house, shower, et al. Won't be able to take much along, I guess.

February 21st ...
Still the rumors persist. No positive indication of a move yet, though. Went to the dentist again today. My teeth are O.K. again.

February 22nd ...
This morning, Guzz, our Section Chief, went with Lt. Kellow for a weeks tour, all secret, but probably to the new field.

FLASH!
Tonight I never saw so much trouble ......
C.V. had an attack of something ... Malaria, appendicitis, poisoning or something. Anyway, he got the cramps so bad we had to take him to the hospital in town. When I got back, Reuss told me I was to leave day after tomorrow for the other

field ... It was 3:00 in the morning ... Holy smoke, what a situation! This house and no one left to tear it down. I'll take off tomorrow and try to disassemble it to a certain extent. Of course, I knew this wasn't exactly permanent here, but I still hate to move if we are only going north in Italy a ways.

February 23rd ...
I really worked today. Disassembled everything I wanted to take along. I took the pipes off the shower and the pictures off the walls, the radio out of the chair and the blankets off the bed. I packed some of C.V.'s stuff as well as my four barracks bags. There isn't enough transportation to take all my picture producing equipment, so I boxed some of the most essential things.

We had a couple of meetings today, telling us when we'll be getting up, eating breakfast, starting, etc. One of the trucks was loaded today, so after supper I put some things on it that I thought I wouldn't be able to take tomorrow. The house is stripped now and doesn't look so good. The shower still stands but is stripped also. I've really been busy tearing down and packing today and am ready for the sack now at 10:30 p.m.

February 24th ...
Got up at 1:00 a.m. this morning and, as suspected, slept very little last night. I rolled up my bed roll and wrapped my comforter around the radio and put it in a barracks bag. After putting all valuables on the truck, we went to breakfast. We had all we wanted to eat ... I had five eggs, cereal with straight canned milk, coffee, and a couple of oranges. That should last 'til noon. As there wasn't enough room for everyone on the truck, Starks and two other fellows and I took a jeep ... better than a truck anyway. At 3:00 a.m. we started out, four other

trucks besides us. It was pretty cold until the sun came up but we had our leather flying clothes on and didn't suffer too much. We went pretty slow until we got to Termoli where the road got better, then we made time.

About this time ... the sun is up now ... we cracked the first bottle of rum we had with us and opened a coke. This makes about the best combination over here as the whiskey, brandy, etc. is terrible. Course, this isn't for the connoisseur. Only three of us are drinking and when we open the second bottle of rum we are very happy we are making the trip. Har, Har, Har. About 11:00 a.m. was the zenith of our folly and when we stopped at 1:00 p.m. to eat, the storm was subsiding.

I drove from below Pescara to the field, arriving here at about 4:00 p.m. It is a really nice trip up here, as the road goes along the sea and at some places excellent views are gotten. The towns seem a little cleaner up here but some are certainly blown up bad, Ancona's harbor, for one place.

The field ... air strip ... is still being constructed and won't be ready for a week or two, I guess. We went to headquarters building when we got here and set up our cots in a room, also connected up the radio. There aren't very many fellows up here now from the group and we should eat pretty good for a while. I suppose we will be doing all kinds of work details while here.

February 25th ...
Had fried eggs and bacon, cereal, bread, coffee, etc. this morning. Good chow. First we went down to where our camp area is to be and unloaded the truck load of barracks bags, bed rolls, etc. There are two buildings (farm houses) that are to be ours as soon as we move the Italians out of them. One is to be for the officers to sleep in, the other is to be an administration building. They are large but very dirty and will need much

cleaning. These houses here have the livestock downstairs and the people live up. Not good from the sanitary angle, but convenient.

I don't know the exact set-up the Government has for these people but I guess they are moved in with other families on other farms and undoubtedly paid rent for the building and land. Most of the people are tenant farmers ... peasants, really ... but being moved out lock, stock and barrel seems wrong, too. C est la guerre, I guess.

We put up three tents for the twelve men and two officers, and I think our bivouac area will be pretty nice. The field isn't too far from the sea ... three quarters of a mile ... and later on we will no doubt be going down swimming quite regularly.

February 26th ...
Today we hauled gravel for walks, mess hall and tents, dug latrine holes, cleaned buildings and other general duties. Worked pretty hard all day. Went to bed at 8:00 p.m. as there is no electricity, and slept good until 6:30 a.m.

February 28th ...
We are still getting the area in shape for the rest of the Squadron ... putting up tents, etc. Tonight after supper the Major wanted us to work 'til dark putting up tents. 'Rip" Pollack and I got some laundry together and took off for an Eytie farmhouse for the evening. When we returned after dark we got hell from the Major for leaving and now everyone has to get permission to leave camp.

March 1st 1945 ...
This morning ... 9:00 a.m. ... a fellow came over from Group and wanted a radio man to help over there, so they asked me to go. Naturally I went as anything is better than

digging a hole. What the job was, was laying telephone lines from Group to the Squadrons and two of us did it. Looks like a few days job. We heard transports might be in with equipment and personnel soon.

March 3rd ...
Some fellows came in today in a truck convoy with some equipment. More by plane tomorrow, I guess.

March 4th ...
Am still laying lines and enjoying it. Some *C-47*'s came in today. If we can keep the room we have an eye on for our radio shop, it will be very nice. Some of the fellows are working on it now ... putting a ceiling in, etc.

March 6th ...
Most of the fellows are here now from the other field and the planes also. I'm back working for the Squadron now. Five of us have moved into a tent together ... Guzz, our radio section chief, Warren Lints (in the orderly room,) Carl Reuss, Doc Savage and Doc Petit (that's me.) Guzz and Doc and I were in houses at the last field so we didn't have anybody to move in with. I connected the radio up but don't know if we'll be able to get Foggia from here or not. Some stations come in O.K. though. We heard today that some of the furlough boys (Vance Lee) are in Italy here somewhere on their way back.

March 7th ...
We made a shower-run to Fano tonight, about twelve miles up the highway. Seems to be many pretty girls here, and the people seem to be cleaner, too. That Foggia area we just came from is, to me, one of the dirtiest I've seen in Italy. Sure glad to leave there. I'd like to get back to Ancona or up to Rimini someday.

March 8th ...

Vance Lee and about eight others arrived today. They look a little dissipated but that's to be expected after forty days or so of U.S. night life. He got engaged. Guess he'll move in here with us. That will make six, and a tent full.

March 11th ...

Tonight we were playing volley ball on our newly constructed court and I turned my ankle in a hole and hurt it pretty bad. I heard something snap ... don't know if there is a bone broken or not. I soaked it in hot water for a while in the aid station. Tomorrow I'll go on sick call.

March 12th ...

My foot hurt terribly this morning when I tried to step on it so I started using crutches I got last night. I went on sick call and then down to Senegalia to a hospital and had it X-rayed. Sure enough, there is a complete fracture of the bone that runs from my little toe up to the ankle socket. What luck. The Doc said I'd be off that foot for a few weeks. That means I go on crutches for a while ... and me planning on a 30-day furlough in June. I certainly hope it is healed by then. The worst part of it is the inconvenience of going on crutches.

March 14th ...

It must be pretty bad when a guy has to use crutches the rest of his life because of a leg or hip injury. Maybe getting used to them is the hardest job. I have to have one of the Yugoslav KP's get my meals (two, as I don't eat breakfast anymore) and wash my mess kit. I go late to chow after nearly everyone has finished.

March 17th ...
Reuss got the radio jeep tonight and we went to a show at Headquarters. Wasn't worth freezing for, I didn't think. The show is outside now as there isn't any room for a theater inside here.

March 20th ...
I've been reading quite a bit lately, that's about all I can do as I'm marked "quarters."

March 27th ...
Pappy Hale's outfit is going to move on this field a little later. They are making another runway now.

March 31st ...
I went to the hospital for another X-ray today, hoping that my foot would be healed O.K.. It wasn't, and I've got at least three weeks more on these crutches. This is no good! There won't be too much time to spare after I start walking again and go home.

April 8th 1945 ...
Today the April bunch of fellows left for home, sort of early but of course they were glad about it. Don't know when my name will be submitted for next month.

April 12th ...
The Doc checked my foot this morning and decided to have another X-ray taken the 21st of this month. It will be nearly six weeks then and I certainly hope O.K..

April 15th ...
Heard my name with six or eight others was submitted today.

April 16th ...

Went with Vance Lee to Fano today to get some crystals. We stopped by the *Red Cross Club* there for coffee and doughnuts. It's sort of a nice trip. Today the weather was swell.

April 21st ...

Went to the hospital in Senegalia this morning and had my foot X-rayed. Had to wait until 1:00 p.m. as there were a lot of fellows there. We had dinner and about 1:30 p.m. the Doc told me to walk. It seemed funny as I hadn't even put my foot down since March 11th. It doesn't hurt to walk a little if I use a cane. I made a cane out of a couple slats and have thrown the crutches away. It is healed O.K., I guess, and I hope in about a week I can walk without any support. Should be healed just in time for when I go home, if we do about May 10th or thereabouts. Now I don't have to have one of the K.P.'s get any meals for me.

April 24th ...

Still hobbling around on a cane. Guess it'll be all right soon.

April 26th ...

This noon Warren told me we furlough men are leaving Sunday (29th) morning for Bari, the first leg of our journey home. I have most of my clothes separated and bagged so I haven't much else to do but turn in what I don't want to take. Hope I don't have to carry my dufflebag far as my foot won't stand too much weight. I'll have to take my cane.

April 27th ...

Today I sent my footlocker and a box of books home.

I certainly hope they all get there. There is quite a bit of stuff in the foot locker. I turned in one barracks bag of clothes, will turn in the rest tomorrow. Wrote some letters tonight, trying to catch up. Had boned chicken on toast tonight, as usual, before going to bed. I'll miss this when I leave.

April 28th ...
Turned in my gun, gas mask, comforter and other extra clothes today. Got a hair cut, a permit for my Mauser rifle, and my old air mattress back. The fellow I sold it to over a year ago still had it and the pillow leaks, so he sold it to me. I gave $5.50 in England for it new, used it for two years and sold it to him for $20. Today I gave him $15 for it, and even though it leaks it is a good souvenir. It kept me from sleeping on the ground all through Africa although if it hadn't been for that I wouldn't have gotten wounded at Korba. It had raised me up just enough to get hit in the hip. I packed the bag I'll take with me and I am ready to go.

NOTE:
Went to Bari and on to Naples for disembarkation. While disposing of unsmoked cigarettes to various street people in Naples, the war in Europe ended.

We soon sailed for the States and, on June 1st 1945, in Fort Dix, New Jersey ... three years, six months and twenty-four days after enlisting in Pittsburgh on November 8th 1941 ... my service life ended. It was quite an experience ... maybe the most memorable four years of a lifetime.

We said, "......now things will be better." So be it!